Eternity

Dedicated to Arthur Stace (1884–1967)

National Library of Australia cataloguing in publication data

Eternity : stories from the emotional heart of Australia.
ISBN 0 8476 9440 21.
I. Stell, Marion K. II. National Museum of Australia.

A823.3

Design: Art Direction Graphic Design, Canberra.
Printing: National Capital Printing, Canberra.

Cover: 'Eternity' by Arthur Stace, c.1960, purchased by the National Museum of Australia 2000. Photograph by George Serras, National Museum of Australia.

Bushrangers, by definition, were outlaws from society, ostracised from the community. Many met their deaths in ill-judged shoot-outs with police. Bushranging was rampant in Australia in the decades from 1860–1890. Not all bushrangers were of convict origin. One, Andrew George Scott — Captain Moonlite — was an educated and intelligent man. He led a gang of six bushrangers: James Nesbitt, Graham Bennett, Thomas Rogan, Thomas Williams and Gus Wreneckie. Moonlite met James Nesbitt in Pentridge Gaol where, according to later reports, 'in order to preserve discipline, [the two] had to be separated. After their release they were inseparable companions.' In November 1879 the gang robbed Wantabadgery station near Wagga, Wagga, NSW, then fled and took refuge in a hut used by the land selector McGlede. Pursuing police shot dead two of the gang, including James Nesbitt. The *Sydney Mail* reported:

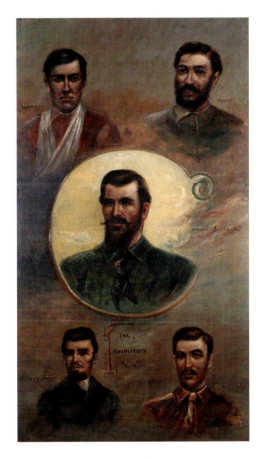

MOONLITE'S GANG WITH JAMES NESBITT AT BOTTOM RIGHT
The Moonliters, 1894, by Patrick William Marony,
National Library of Australia

Nesbitt, though shot through the temple so badly that his brains protruded, lived for fully half-an-hour, during which time Moonlite manifested much grief at the dying man's fate ... It is said that all the time Nesbitt was lying in McGlede's kitchen with the bullet wound in his head and dying, Moonlite wept over him like a child, laid his head upon the dying man's breast and kissed him passionately.

From prison, waiting to be hanged, Moonlite penned a number of letters with the dual purpose of explaining his actions and expressing his desire not to be separated from Nesbitt in death:

We were hardly dealt with, we were weary of all we had suffered, and weak with hunger. Privation and despair conquered reason; we were sorely tempted and fell. My dearest Jim in his death showed the noble charity of his nature, he kept me from shedding blood and shed no blood himself. When he died my heart was crushed. I never found a better friend, or a truer man. My fondest hope is to be with him in Eternity and that I may share his grave. As to the monumental stone for my friend and myself. A rough unhewn rock would be the most fit, one that skilled hands could have made into something better. It will be like those it covers, as Kindness and Charity could have shaped us to better ends.

AG SCOTT, 1880

Moonlite's letters were intercepted and none reached their destination. The two men were buried separately. In 1995 Moonlite and Nesbitt were re-buried together in a cemetery in Gundagai, NSW.

In the 1880s it was thought that criminals could be identified by phrenology — through the shape of their skull and head.

CAPTAIN MOONLITE'S DEATH MASK,
JUSTICE AND POLICE MUSEUM, SYDNEY
George Serras, National Museum of Australia

SOURCES AND FURTHER READING: *Town and Country Journal*, 22 November 1879; *Sydney Mail*, 22 November 1879;
Stephan Williams (ed), *The Moonlite Papers*, Popinjay, Woden, 1991.

GERTRUD BODENWIESER
Bodenwieser Collection, National Library of Australia

Modern dance exponent and acclaimed choreographer Gertrud Bodenwieser was forced to flee her native Vienna in 1938. Her husband and family were murdered. She brought her dance troupe to Australia. She felt keenly her separation from homeland, culture and family. Acclaimed the 'pioneer of the living dance', Gertrud Bodenwieser left few writings herself. Much that we know about her comes from recollections by her students and colleagues:

GERTRUD BODENWIESER
Bodenweiser Collection, National Library of Australia

A few decades are still likely to pass, before the contribution made by Bodenwieser to both Australian and New Zealand theatre and dance is fully understood. Certainly the twenty-one years of her exile wrought changes in Bodenwieser herself, without which she could never have made the contributions she did to the cultural scene. But the real 'Bodie' did not change for us who knew her best. The 'keine kultur', (no culture) syndrome which she bemoaned so much in the beginning did not alter very much but she learned to keep it to herself, or at least within her own circle of continental friends. Some may have considered her an intellectual snob. One had to admit she often sounded like one, but for someone who in better days had moved among the most famous and most avant-garde artists of her time, it could not have been otherwise. By comparison, the intrinsic lack of trained minds, and keen intellects in the new world in which she now found herself must have seemed hardship indeed.

I had stood in great awe of Frau Gerty in Vienna, yet I felt far closer to her now, witnessing her vulnerability in this raw new country — a vulnerability which contrasted so strikingly with the remote and rather formidable figure to whom we had curtsied at the Academy in Vienna murmuring 'Kuss die Hand, gnadige Frau,' (I kiss your hand, gracious lady). Australians did not pride themselves upon that sort of old world courtesy, and it must have taken some time for Frau Gerty to adjust to their easy egalitarianism. They, in turn, were sometimes baffled by her foreign ways and intensity of spirit ... Although Frau Gerty remained something of an enigma to many of her students who were incapable of understanding the complexities of her past, few would deny their indebtedness to her for the enrichment of their own lives.

Artistic nomads of Australia, the Bodenwieser Ballet covered thousands of miles and danced for all sorts of people from many walks of life. We danced for the initiated in the Capital cities in many States, but also opened the eyes of people in remote areas and won the enthusiasm of many a former sceptic.

SHONA DUNLOP MACTAVISH, 1987

GERTRUD BODENWIESER'S STAGE GOWN,
NATIONAL MUSEUM OF AUSTRALIA
Gerald Preiss, National Museum of Australia

SOURCES AND FURTHER READING: Shona Dunlop MacTavish, *An Ecstasy of Purpose: The Life and Art of Gertrud Bodenwieser*, Les Humphrey and Associates, Dunedin, NZ, 1987.

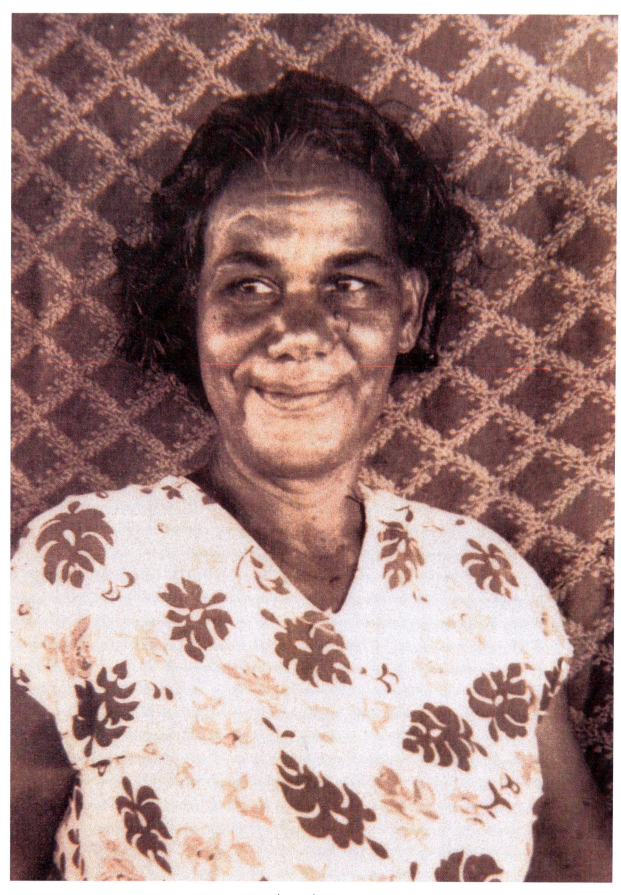

Isabella Lynott
On loan from Pearl Hamaguchi

Pearl Hamaguchi, Isabella Lynott's niece, delivered the following eulogy at the Thanksgiving Eucharist to celebrate the life of Isabella Lynott at Our Lady Queen of Peace Cathedral Broome, on 26 October 1998.

BEAGLE BAY MISSION
Grant Sellwood

Aunty Bella was born at Ruby Station, east of Halls Creek. In 1909 when she was 7 years old, she was put on a horse drawn cart, together with her little sister Barbara aged 4, and her cousins Margaret, Ruby, Wilhelmena and George Button, all of whom were not much older. Mr Robert Button, the station owner of Ruby Plains accompanied them as far as Wyndham, where other children from the Kimberley were waiting to start their journey into the unknown. Aunty Bella remembered every detail of that journey: the wailing mothers, the terrifying feeling of being on a boat in the ocean while being seasick and hungry. She had never seen the sea or a boat before. Throughout the journey she protected her little sister.

After arriving at Broome, weak and fainting, their journey continued to Beagle Bay. Aunty Bella spoke with fondness about arriving at Beagle Bay. She was so weak from the journey, she had to be carried by Fr. Bishoffs from the boat to the Mission. On arrival she was allotted her bed in the 'little girls' dormitory. She attended school, was baptised and learnt about God. The years went by, then she became a 'middle size girl', and eventually a 'big girl'.

It was the big girls' job to help the nuns care for the 'little girls' who kept coming from the Kimberley. Aunty Bella took this job on with great dedication; no other interest distracted her. It turned out that this was what she was chosen to do for the next 40 years of her life. After the war she moved from Beagle Bay to Broome, where she cared for and loved the girls at the Orphanage.

Aunty Bella was a person of simplicity. She never wanted to be burdened by materialism. She always had great pleasure in giving away gifts as soon as she received them. Her deep love and concern continued as her immediate and extended families grew into the hundreds with her orphanage girls now becoming grandparents.

Please God, we pray that all of us here today will be blessed by her life and death. May she be an example to us throughout our lives.

May she rest in Peace.

PEARL HAMAGUCHI, 1998

NAIDOC TROPHY AWARDED TO ISABELLA LYNOTT,
PEARL HAMAGUCHI
George Serras, National Museum of Australia

SOURCES AND FURTHER READING: Pearl Hamaguchi, 'Auntie Bella's story', in *Thanksgiving Eucharist to Celebrate the Life of Isabella Lynott, 1902–1998*, Our Lady Queen of Peace Cathedral Broome, 26 October 1998.

JESSIE VASEY
National Library of Australia

Jessie Vasey felt the anguish of inconsolable grief after the death of her husband, Major General George (Alan) Vasey, when his plane crashed into the sea off Cairns in 1945. The same year she formed the War Widows' Guild and was its president for 21 years until her own death in 1966. Towards the end of her life she finished working a tapestry begun when the family was living in India in 1936. It depicted a happier family time. She wrote this letter to thousands of war widows in 1945; it touched each personally.

JESSIE VASEY (SECOND FROM LEFT) FAREWELLS HER HUSBAND IN DECEMBER 1939
Australian War Memorial

During my long connection with soldiers' families I have felt, always, that the sacrifice demanded of the war widow and her family by the community was a terrible one. In spite of my hopes and efforts very little has been done for them, especially for that group of women for whom living on a beggarly pittance will mean a complete alteration in their way of life. It hurt my husband very much that the families of the men he had loved so greatly, the men who had died uncomplainingly for Australia, should suffer privation and want because of that sacrifice. Our last evening together was spent in discussing ways of improving their conditions with some of our friends, and then General Vasey said: 'Stick to the war widows now and when I come back you shall have every atom of help I can give you. To me, their position is incredible, surely their loss is itself more than enough to suffer'. My husband never came back to give me that help, but his words remain for me the goal at which I aim and at which I hope the War Widows' Guild will aim — 'their loss itself is more than enough to suffer'.

For a long time I felt that real help for widows could only come from among themselves, now, as one of them, I am sure of it. It is only the women who have faced the problems and the terrors of that long walk in the shadows who can understand what the other widow must face and know how to give her a helping hand. In grief and bewilderment we must all grope for some meaning to life; for me the anchor to which I cling is the thought that I must go on, that I must not be a drag on the victory for which my husband laid down his life.

During the long and difficult years of the war women have shouldered heavy burdens; the war widow may never lay hers down. Yet it is no mean destiny to be called upon to go on for a man who has laid down his life, as Christ did, to save mankind from the power of the Beast. Our husbands fought against hopeless odds and overcame them; we can do the same for, from their sacrifice, will come our strength. It rests with us, the war widows, to make our Guild a power in the land.

JESSIE VASEY, 1945

JESSIE VASEY'S TAPESTRY, ROBERT VASEY
George Serras, National Museum of Australia

SOURCES AND FURTHER READING: Mavis Thorpe Clark, *No Mean Destiny: The Story of the War Widows' Guild of Australia 1945–85*, Hyland House, Melbourne, 1986.

PRINCE LEONARD
Courtesy WA Newspapers

On 21 April 1970 Leonard George Casley served formal notice on the Premier and the Governor of Western Australia, the Acting Prime Minister, Sir John McEwen, and the Governor-General, Sir Paul Hasluck, that his land was to be the Hutt River Province and that he was to be its administrator. In a further application of bush law he changed the province to a principality and declared himself Prince Leonard and his wife Princess Shirley. He had successfully seceded from Australia. Casley was reacting to what he regarded as an unfair wheat quota set by the Western Australian government. He turned his 18,500-acre property near Geraldton into a tourist mecca, printing his own stamps, passports and currency, and adopting all the trappings of a real principality. Over the years Prince Leonard has made his concerns known through the Australian media.

On that quota it would have taken me about 50 years to grow as much wheat as I did the year before. At the same time the general public may have considered it a joke but I certainly did not.

SUNDAY TELEGRAPH, 26 January 1975

Ours is the only government speaking for the people of this territory, and ours is a government of self-preservation. We must be recognised.

BULLETIN, 17 May 1975

Neither West Australia nor Australia has any jurisdiction in Hutt River.

WOMAN'S DAY, 31 May 1976

I wish that relations between us could be more cordial — after all Hutt River Province is the second-largest country in this continent. Australia could be a more neighbourly neighbour.

CANBERRA TIMES, 30 August 1976

People who visit the province are with us in spirit. I have done something a lot of people would like to do.

AGE, 29 March 1977

This is no joke you know. People thought it was a joke when we started. I don't think they do now. By addressing me in letters as the Prince, governments have acknowledged that we exist.

ADVERTISER, 6 January 1978

The constitution provides me with $1 a year as the ruler. This is to confirm that I am a constitutionally-approved head of State, thereby preventing future dictatorships. However, the monarchy will be hereditary instead of an elected one. The heir to the throne will be my eldest son, Prince Ian, who is at present Minister for Social Services.

AUSTRALIAN, 24 April 1980

Everything we've done has been within the law.

WHO WEEKLY, 22 March 1999

When I was born it was into the British Empire. It was a mighty empire but it's not now — so any empire can crumble in just one lifetime.

WHO WEEKLY, 22 March 1999

PRINCESS SHIRLEY AND PRINCE LEONARD
Courtesy WA Newspapers

FIRST DAY COVER

HUTT RIVER PROVINCE stamps
George Serras, National Museum of Australia

SOURCES AND FURTHER READING: Robert Hyslop, *The Man: His Royal Highness Prince Leonard, Sovereign of the Hutt River Province Principality,* LG Casley, Hutt River, WA, 1979.

A crime has been committed by an unknown assassin,
within a short distance of the principal streets of this great
city, and is surrounded by an impenetrable mystery.

FERGUS HUME, 1886

There is something elusive and mysterious
in this land, some soul that I cannot find,
some spirit I have never seen,
something I can only feel.

EB MACKENNAL, 1927

Even the mystery of possession is a mystery
that it is not possible to share.

PATRICK WHITE, 1955

AUSTRALIA was the last of the great continents to yield up
the contours of its coastline to the map of the world ... the
new Southern land had remained much of a mystery to the
adventurous mariners of Europe. It was a period of discovery
following on a still greater era of romantic exploration of seas
unknown. Dutch, French, Spanish, Portuguese, they had all
seen (and sailed away again) some portion of the shoreline
of the mysterious continent.

MARY E FULLERTON, 1928

In the mist
You'd hear knuckle-bones rattle
in their cotton pockets; or darned
in conversation, obscene words, slurred
by badly brewed alcohol; never song
but garbled recitations, coughed half-chants.

ROBERT ADAMSON, 2000

MYSTERY

An elusive knot lies at the heart of any good mystery.
What draws us in are the secrets and lies, the intrigue
and talk of conspiracy.
No matter how many times we tell the story, wonder
what really happened, what might have been,
questions remain.
Not everything can be explained.
The enigma, in the end, is something you feel.

FRANCESCA RENDLE-SHORT, 2000

Silence ruled this land.
Out of silence mystery
comes, and magic and
the delicate awareness
of unreasoning things.

ELEANOR DARK, 1941

Destiny has four feet—
eight hands, and
sixteen eyes.
So how can a
poooorrrr mortaaaaaal   eeeeeevil-doeeeeer
with only two of each
hope to escape?

BETH YAHP, 2000

Their paths crossed, and
diverged, and met, and
knotted. Their mystery
of purpose had found the
solution to the mystery
of silence.

PATRICK WHITE, 1955

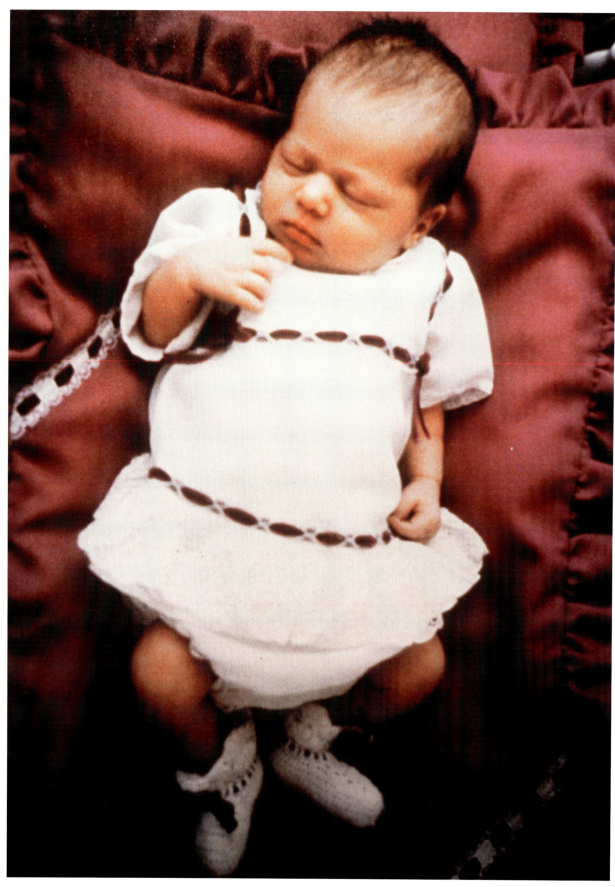

AZARIA CHAMBERLAIN
Sydney Freelance/Chamberlain

Baby Azaria Chamberlain lived for only 68 days, but the mystery of her disappearance from her parents' tent at the Uluru (Ayers Rock) camp site in the Northern Territory has fascinated the nation for more than 20 years. Her body was never found and the coroner's inquest concluded that she had been taken by a dingo, as her parents, Lindy and Michael Chamberlain, claimed. Bizarre stories and speculation spread like wildfire, fuelled by unfamiliarity with her parents' religion, Seventh-Day Adventists, and the fact that Azaria had been seen dressed in black. A second inquest changed the finding and in 1982 Lindy was sentenced to life imprisonment. This was eventually quashed and both parents were pardoned. In 1990 Lindy Chamberlain wrote *Through My Eyes*.

MICHAEL AND LINDY CHAMBERLAIN
AFTER THE FIRST INQUEST
Courtesy *Canberra Times*/National Library of Australia

This is the story of a little girl

who lived, and breathed, and loved, and was loved.

She was part of me.

She grew within my body and when she died,

part of me died,

And nothing will ever alter that fact ...

We must fight for the preservation of discerning laws in this country. One day I was just a happy housewife and mother, known only to my friends and acquaintances, next day a household word. I never dreamed it could possibly happen to me — how about you? If this continues will you be next?

How do you think we felt knowing most of you, our fellow Australians, were often maliciously discussing us over the morning coffee? It is amazing when one sets out to spread a rumour about another, just how quickly that rumour can take hold. Certainly the old adage that 'a lie goes round the world while truth puts its boots on', is a very accurate description of what happened in our case. But truth's boots can be big and crushing when they're on — and those boots just keep right on walking.

No matter how many years down the track it may be or how much they've proved to be untrue, it is still mind-boggling how some of these rumours started and were believed. How gullible people can be when lies are put over in a plausible way! We still hear these rumours coming back to us, although they have been discredited time and again.

LINDY CHAMBERLAIN, 1990

The media often misquoted me. They made up all sorts of dreadful stories. That Azaria was a sacrifice. That we always dressed her in black. One of the media misquotes was that Azaria meant Bearer of Sin.

LINDY CHAMBERLAIN, 2000

BABY AZARIA'S BLACK DRESS,
NATIONAL MUSEUM OF AUSTRALIA
George Serras, National Museum of Australia

SOURCES AND FURTHER READING: Lindy Chamberlain, *Through My Eyes*, William Heinemann, Port Melbourne, 1990.

GRANNY LOCKE
Peter Knowles, Boulia Shire Council

The mysterious Min Min Lights have been seen by many people in outback Queensland. Most of the sightings are around the central Queensland town of Boulia. Granny Jean Locke has personally seen them on four separate occasions. No satisfactory scientific explanation exists to account for them.

TOWN SIGN, BOULIA, QLD
Boulia Shire Council

The longest I've seen the Min Min Light — I went to Bedourie for a gymkhana with my daughter — to ride back with her. We left at half past ten that night. Didn't get far out of Bedourie when a light appeared over the side of us. But I knew there was a lot of roads out there so it was a car with one light. But then we came to a gidgee scrub and the Min Min Light was still there and I knew there was no roads whatsoever through there. And it was about 100 yards off the road and it was about four foot off the ground. And it didn't matter how fast we went it'd stop level with us. It's moving all the time like a car going over the ground but there's no reflection out the front like a car light, it's just a light and it followed us all the way within 26 miles of here.

The other time I saw this Min Min Light we thought it was a spotlight up the paddock and we drove up there, it was there till we nearly got there and then all of a sudden it disappeared. But we couldn't find a car track or anything so it couldn't have been anyone up there spotlighting. It had to have a car so we presumed that was the Min Min light too.

Nobody can take a photograph of it, plenty of people have tried, and when they get the film developed there's always blanks where the photos of the Min Min Light was taken. One woman took five photographs, and five of them were black.

It can't be a bird, it can't be gas what they reckon. Because how could it stay with that car when it went as fast as it did. So I wouldn't know what it is, wouldn't have a clue, what do you reckon it is? Probably black fellas knew it before we did and that's why they're frightened of it.

GRANNY LOCKE, 1999

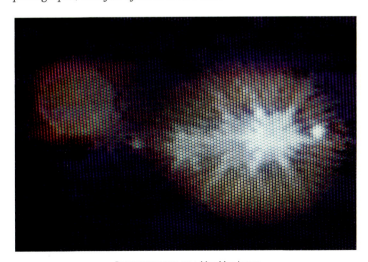

REPRESENTATION OF A MIN MIN LIGHT
George Serras, National Museum of Australia

SOURCES AND FURTHER READING: Granny Locke, interview with Jason Webb, 1999, Promotion Pictures, Mansfield; Maureen G Kozicka, *The Mystery of the Min Min Light*, self-published, Mt Molloy, 1994.

HAROLD HOLT
Courtesy *Age*

Many theories exist to explain the mysterious vanishing of Australia's eighteenth prime minister, Harold Holt, at Cheviot Beach, Portsea, Victoria, on 17 December 1967. One of them was told by Holt's friend Peter Lynch, and surfaced in an article by Alan Dearn in the *Melbourne Herald* in 1982.

CHEVIOT
Courtesy Nepean History Society

Six skindivers, including Australia's Prime Minister Mr Harold Holt, tampered with the sunken wreck of the passenger steamer Cheviot off Portsea, unaware that 28 souls were entombed in the hulk since 1887. The six frogmen have each faced brushes with death since then — and four have died.

Much fantasy surrounds the death of Harold Holt — including one incredible suggestion that he was taken at sea by a spy submarine — but the strangest story of all is 'the curse of the Cheviot'.

These four, who each met an unnatural death while they were unaccompanied, kept brass porthole fittings off the Cheviot as mementos of their diving adventure. The other two have survived brushes with death ... when they were not alone.

'There was light-hearted discussion in our social group, and I remember the jinx being discussed. We joked about the jinx and I said to Harold Holt "You're next, Harold!" He just laughed at the suggestion. He had the same attitude as the rest of us who disturbed the shipwreck. We were unconcerned and mildly amused at superstitious talk of retribution.'

Mr Lynch has no doubt that Harold Holt's death a month later was 'just a drowning, a tragic loss, but the sort of thing that does happen.'

He believes Mr Holt was held down in bull kelp, lost his mask and snorkel, and became disorientated.

But an air of mystery still surrounds his disappearance.

Mr Lynch's story stems from the loss of the steamer Cheviot with 35 dead, described by historians as 'the most tragic wreck ever to occur in the vicinity of Port Phillip Heads.'

Seven bodies were recovered. The remaining 28 were left entombed in the sunken fore part of the ship, which lost its propeller in a storm outside the Heads.

Mr Lynch said that for a brief period every few years the stern half of the Cheviot became visible on extremely low tide about 100 metres off Portsea.

'When the six of us dived on the wreck early in 1963 we were unaware that it was decided back in the 1880s to leave the bodies there.'

'There has been plenty of macabre talk about retribution for disturbing the resting place of the Cheviot.'

MELBOURNE HERALD, 31 JULY 1982

PORTHOLE FROM THE CHEVIOT RETRIEVED BY HAROLD HOLT, NEPEAN HISTORICAL SOCIETY AND NICHOLAS HOLT
George Serras, National Museum of Australia

SOURCES AND FURTHER READING: *Melbourne Herald*, 31 July 1982, reproduced courtesy Herald & Weekly Times.

THE GREAT LEVANTE
Performing Arts Museum, Victorian Arts Centre

Leslie George Cole, The Great Levante, was Australia's greatest escapologist and magician. Born in Junee in country New South Wales, he toured the world performing illusions and magic tricks. His troupe entertained Australian soldiers in London during the Second World War. He was adept at escape, a skill evident in his description of a jump off Lambeth Bridge in London in 1933.

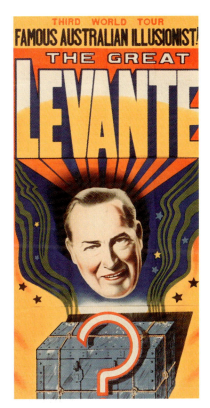

Performing Arts Museum, Victorian Arts Centre

I'm standing on the rail of the Lambeth Bridge which crosses the Thames. Behind me Big Ben has just chimed twelve o'clock and here I am in a bathing costume, having been duly leg-ironed, handcuffed with two pairs of police handcuffs and a chain locked around my neck. The end of the chain runs down and is attached with another lock to the handcuffs. The end of the chain is locked to the leg-irons. The chain is really for no other purpose than to keep the handcuffs and the leg-irons together for I am about to jump into the Thames from a height of about forty feet and to make an escape under water. Presently, I feel a hand grab me around the ankle. I look down and there is a young London policeman, complete with helmet, a coat over his arm and he said to me, 'Have you permission to do this, sir?' I said, 'Yes.' He said, 'May I see it?' ... I duly made the jump ...

I ran down to the hotel and as I went into the passageway I saw a lot of the press boys there and I said to them, 'I don't think we have permission to do this dive and this young policeman is going to pinch me.'

With that I went upstairs and had a hot bath and about some thirty minutes later I came down to be greeted by the press and the young policeman, and I have never in my life seen a policeman get so drunk so quickly. Those press boys had just poured hot rum and hot water into him and he was 'non-compos'. I have never heard any more about it since.

Leslie Cole, 1973

The Great Levante performed the illusion 'Sawing a Woman in Half':

... the girl was tied at the wrists, throat and ankles, the ropes were passed out through the holes in the sides of the box. The box was standing in the centre of the stage and then laid down onto trestles and the lid closed. Through it were passed sheets of steel and a couple of sheets of glass, showing that the box was divided into eight equal parts. Then the box was cut across the middle with a cross-cut saw while the ropes were held by a committee from the audience ... in my mind, this illusion was one of the best ever invented because it had a thrill; it could be done anywhere, completely surrounded and, in addition, it had the feminine angle and it was more or less foolproof.

Leslie Cole, 1973

Cross-cut saw from the illusion 'Sawing a Woman in Half', Performing Arts Museum, Melbourne George Serras, National Museum of Australia

SOURCES AND FURTHER READING: Kent Blackmore, *Levante: His Life, No Illusion*, Mike Caveney's Magic Words, Pasadena, 1997.

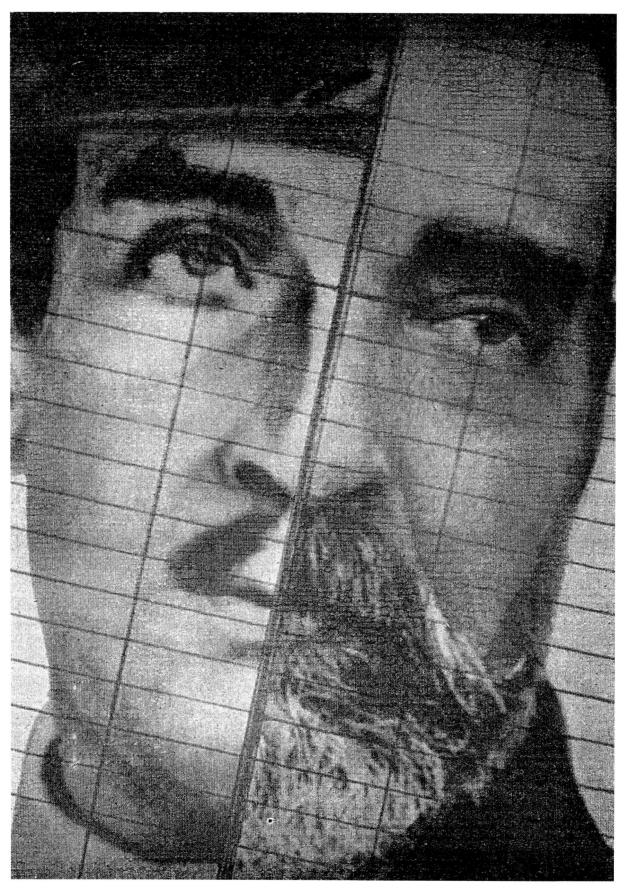

TICHBORNE/CLAIMANT
Courtesy Wagga Wagga City Library

The Tichborne Claimant
1829 (1834?) – 1898

In 1865 an advertisement appeared in the *Sydney Morning Herald* offering a handsome reward for information regarding the fate of Roger Charles Doughty Tichborne who had sailed from South America in 1864 and had not been heard of since. He was a baronet and heir to the English Tichborne estates. A butcher from Wagga Wagga, NSW, previously known as Tom Castro, but also going by the name of Arthur Orton, claimed to be the lost heir. He and his wife travelled to England and were reunited with his mother, Lady Tichborne, and moved into the Tichborne estates. Other members of the family, however, were not as certain and the case went to trial. Without clear means to establish identity, and before photographs were commonplace, many ingenious ways were used to determine whether the Claimant was legitimate — the size of ears, face comparisons, noses, thumbs, handwriting and tattoos remembered from long ago. The case caught the popular imagination in both England and Australia. The Claimant was found not to be Tichborne and so was tried for perjury. He was convicted and sent to prison, but when he died, the family consented to him being buried in the Tichborne vaults as Roger Tichborne. Was he the heir after all?

THE CLAIMANT
National Library of Australia

Dr Kenealy MP represented the Claimant. Following the trial he went on a lecture tour of England where he made this speech:

I was nearly 50 days addressing the Court of Queen's Bench; and even in that long time I did not attempt to unriddle the thousand and one enigmas to be found in the career of the Defendant. The claimant himself is the greatest enigma that ever the world saw. If he is TICHBORNE, it is a mystery of mysteries how he could have committed the wonderful follies of which he was guilty. If he is not TICHBORNE, but a pretender, it is, and ever will continue to be a wonder of the world, while the world lasts, how he could persuade noblemen, gentlemen, ladies, priests, carabineers, constituting of some of the finest soldiers in the world, nearly all of the old tenants on the Tichborne estate, and lastly, Lady TICHBORNE, one of the keenest, cleverest, and most suspicious women that ever lived, that he was no other than the long-lost ROGER; the long-absent son; the heir who had been missed for so many weary years.

DR KENEALY MP, 1880

SOUVENIR FIGURES FROM THE TICHBORNE TRIAL — LADY TICHBORNE, THE CHIEF JUSTICE, THE CLAIMANT, DR KENEALY, MUSEUM OF THE RIVERINA
George Serras, National Museum of Australia

SOURCES AND FURTHER READING: *The Trial at the Bar of Sir Roger CD Tichborne, Bart, in the Court of Queen's Bench at Westminster ...* , Englishman Office, London, 1875–1880, vols 9–10.

The joy and hope the swagman feels
   Returning, after shearing,
Or after six months' tramp Out Back,
   He strikes the final clearing.
His weary spirit breathes again,
   His aching legs seem limber
When to the East across the plain
   He spots the Darling Timber!

HENRY LAWSON, 1900

He was his father's only hope,
   his mother's pride and joy,
And dearly did his parents love
   their wild colonial boy.

ANONYMOUS, 1905

They had been brought to the last extremity of hope,
and yet they put their hands on each other's shoulders
and said with a passionate conviction that it would be
all right, though they had faith in nothing, but in
themselves and in each other.

FREDERIC MANNING, 1929

Hope is an illusion for squares.

COLIN JOHNSON/MUDROOROO, 1965

Every time I enter a classroom or university lecture
theatre to speak on Aboriginal history, culture and
politics, it leaves me quite breathless because the
students are always so hungry to know about us,
the indigenous first peoples of this land.

DR RUBY LANGFORD GINIBI, 2000

hope

To hope is to dream. Of what might or will be.
Of the possible and the mere possible —
hope against hope. To hope is to strive for the best.
To build on glimmers of new beginnings.
To hope is to never give up.
To remain expectant, against hopes dashed,
disappointments, falsities.
To hope is to believe there is a way.

FRANCESCA RENDLE-SHORT, 2000

The future will not look like
us. Under our ancient
vanished cities they will find
a photograph of the burning
girl, some celluloid with
Katherine Hepburn's smile
on it. And what will they
think of us?

CHRISTOS TSIOLKAS, 2000

I want to have a cold climate chosen for
the capital of this Commonwealth. I want
to have a climate where men can hope.
We cannot have hope in hot countries.

KING O'MALLEY, 1903

For pleasures melt away like snows,
And hopes like shadows glide.

ADAM LINDSAY GORDON, 1893

ARTHUR PHILLIP

The Pioneer by H Macbeth-Raeburn, 1936, National Library of Australia

Arthur Phillip
1738–1814

The First Fleet of convicts arrived in Sydney in 1788 under the command of Governor Arthur Phillip. The new governor was impressed by what he encountered.

This harbour is, in extent and security, very superior to any other that I have ever seen ... The climate is a very fine one, and the country will, I make no doubt, when the woods are cleared away, be as healthy as any in the world ... this country will prove the most valuable acquisition Great Britain ever made.

ARTHUR PHILLIP, 1788

The following year Phillip sent samples of clay found in the new colony back to England where they were fashioned into medallions by Josiah Wedgwood using a design by Henry Webber. They were returned to Phillip who expressed his pleasure that 'Wedgwood has showed the world that our Welch clay is capable of receiving an Elegant impression.' Erasmus Darwin penned a dedicatory poetic response to the medallions.

Visit of Hope
To
Sydney-Cove
Near Botany-Bay
Where Sydney Cove her lucid bosom swells,
Courts her young navies, and the storm repels;
High on a rock amid the troubled air
HOPE stood sublime, and wav'd her golden hair;
Calm'd with her rosy smile the tossing deep,
And with sweet accents charm'd the winds to sleep;
To each wild plain she stretch'd her snowy hand,
High-waving wood, and sea-encircled strand.
'Hear me,' she cried, 'ye rising Realms! record
'Time's opening scenes, and Truth's unerring word —
'There shall broad streets their stately walls extend,
'The circus widen, and the crescent bend;
'There, ray'd from cities o'er the cultur'd land,
Shall bright canals, and solid roads expand. —
'There the proud arch, Colossus-like, bestride
'Yon glittering streams, and bound the chafing tide;
'Embellish'd villas crown the landscape-scene,
'Farms wave with gold, and orchards blush between. —
'There shall tall spires, and dome-capt towers ascend,
'And piers and quays their massy structures blend;
'While with each breeze approaching vessels glide,
'And northern treasures dance on every tide!' —
The ceas'd the nymph-tumultuous echoes roar,
And JOY's loud voice was heard from shore to shore —
Her graceful steps descending press'd the plain,
And PEACE, and ART, and LABOUR, join'd her train.

ERASMUS DARWIN, 1789

THE FIRST FLEET ENTERING BOTANY BAY
Botany Bay, Sirius and Convoy ..., 1788, by William Bradley,
Image Library, State Library of New South Wales

'ETRURIA' OR 'SYDNEY COVE' MEDALLION, C.1790,
MADE BY WEDGWOOD, MITCHELL LIBRARY,
STATE LIBRARY OF NEW SOUTH WALES

SOURCES AND FURTHER READING: FM Blayden (ed), *Historical Records of New South Wales*, vol 1, part 2, *Phillip 1783–1792*, Lansdown Slattery, Mona Vale, 1978; Arthur Phillip, letter to Joseph Banks, 26 July 1790, Series 37.12, Sir Joseph Banks papers, Mitchell Library; James Auchmuty (ed), *The Voyage of Governor Phillip to Botany Bay, with Contributions by Other Officers of the First Fleet*, Angus & Robertson, Sydney, 1970.

BETTY CUTHBERT
Herald & Weekly Times Photographic Collection

28

Betty Cuthbert
born 1938

Seventeen-year-old sprinter Betty Cuthbert won a remarkable haul of three gold medals at the 1956 Melbourne Olympic Games in the 100 metres, 200 metres and the 4 x 100 metres relay. She was hampered by injury at the 1960 Olympics but, encouraged by her coach June Ferguson, she prepared for the longer 400 metres at the 1964 Tokyo Olympics. She built up her stamina on a running machine, then a rarity in Australia. The running machine could be used to train in wet weather, allowed her coach closer scrutiny of her style, improved her balance and endurance, and replicated the feeling of sheer speed. Her main rivals in the race were Australia's Judy Amoore and Great Britain's Ann Packer.

BETTY CUTHBERT'S GOLD MEDAL, 1964 TOKYO OLYMPICS
Herald & Weekly Times Photographic Collection

I got a wonderful start and went flat out as soon as I straightened up. For the first 100 metres I gave it everything I had and was gaining on Judy with every stride. She was the only one I was worried about at that stage. Ann would come later. As we raced down the back straight I felt the wind whip in behind me. Judy must have sensed me right at her heels because she spurted off a yard or so. I let her go. I told myself not to get flurried and to stick to my plan. I was having that little mental breather before really turning it on. Before I knew it we were coming to the curve. I caught Judy going into the bend, about 180 metres from home.

Then I saw Ann for the first time. She seemed way ahead across there in her outside lane and was running well. But I didn't feel tired. Now's the time, I thought to myself. Let it go. I mustered every drop of speed I had in me and turned it loose. I straightened up for that last long drag to the finishing line. I was just in front. Out of the corner of my eye I could see Ann just a fraction behind me. Then the wind hit us. It was like running into a brick wall, but I was determined not to let it straighten me up and kept telling myself to lean forward into it.

I could still see Ann. The wind was terrible and was like an invisible hand pushing against me. I was awfully tired then but forced myself to keep driving ahead. I didn't think it would ever come to an end. My legs were getting heavier as the line edged closer. I wondered how Ann was going and if she had the strength to catch me. By then I knew either Ann or myself was going to win. I felt her right on my heels and knew she must have been just as tired as I was. But I wasn't going to be the first to give in and kept ploughing ahead for all I was worth. Keep going I said to myself ... hold her off ... it's not far now. Ten yards, nine yards, eight yards ... Then there I was just a stride from the tape. I knew I'd done it. I'd won!

All those months and months of training had proved their value in exactly 52 seconds. It was the fastest I'd ever run for the distance and was only a tenth of a second outside Sin Kim Dan's world record. In less than a minute everything I'd planned for, worked for and prayed for HAD come true.

BETTY CUTHBERT, 1966

RUNNING MACHINE USED BY BETTY CUTHBERT,
NATIONAL MUSEUM OF AUSTRALIA
Gerald Preiss, National Museum of Australia

SOURCES AND FURTHER READING: Jim Webster, *Betty Cuthbert, Golden Girl*, Pelham, London, 1966.

NITA GILVEAR
On loan from Nita Gilvear

Nita Gilvear grew up in West Scottsdale in the north-east of Tasmania. A frightening epidemic of polio hit Tasmania in 1937–1938. Polio destroyed Nita's biceps muscle in her arms as well as the muscle that holds the shoulders in their socket. She spent four years in hospital.

NITA GILVEAR IN ARM SPLINTS
On loan from Nita Gilvear

The news items every morning in the papers were reporting about children getting sick with poliomyelitis. Very few people had ever heard of it, except people in the medical profession and they confessed to knowing very little about how to treat this crippling disease which paralysed your limbs and affected the lungs in many cases.

Polio reached epidemic proportions and many children died. The Infectious Diseases Hospital was overflowing. All we talked about at school was polio. The teachers told us to wear camphor in a little bag round our neck. If anyone felt sick or had a headache we had to report immediately to the teacher. Of course there's always panic rumours spread in these situations.

Some of the older children told us stories, I suppose just to dramatise the situation. Things like 'your limbs turn black and you just drop dead in the street'. But of course, these things were not true but we didn't know that.

In November the schools all closed ... About a week after the schools closed I didn't feel very well ... I took the basket and the money for the bread. It seemed such a long way that morning and my legs felt strange ... On my way back with the bread I just didn't know how I was going to get back to the house, or even up the back steps. The footpath seemed to be moving and looked to be waving up and down in front of me. Everything seemed so unreal and I felt so sick I started to vomit in the street.

When I finally got back to the house Auntie Ethel put me to bed. I told her I felt sick, I just wanted to sleep for a while, which I did. When I woke up I had pains in my arms and legs and felt very hot. Even though I felt so ill it never entered my mind that I had polio.

When I eventually became aware of my surroundings I was in a big ward with lots of other children. I knew I was in hospital and I didn't know what happened to me. My arms and legs felt heavy, I hurt all over and every time anyone walked near my bed the vibration sent pains shooting through my whole body and tears would run down my face.

As the days went by I became aware of my surroundings. Lots and lots of beds everywhere with so many children and, the worse thing of all, all those boxes on the other side of the ward. I'd heard people talk about coffins but had never seen one, so I thought they were coffins with dead children, but I couldn't understand why their heads were sticking out. I was terrified and I couldn't ask, and I thought they might put me in one.

I gradually got my voice back and asked about the boxes on the other side of the room. Of course, they were respirators, commonly known as the Iron Lung, to help children breathe.

[Later] I heard someone play an auto-harp on the radio so I decided to get one and learn to play. I advertised in the Scottsdale paper for the instrument and a lady gave me one on the condition that, when I could play it, I go and play it for her, which I did.

I became known as the girl with the harp (not that crippled Lawes girl).

NITA LAWES-GILVEAR, 1988

NITA GILVEAR'S AUTO-HARP, NITA GILVEAR
George Serras, National Museum of Australia

SOURCES AND FURTHER READING: Nita Lawes-Gilvear, *Living with Polio: The Laughter and the Tears*, self-published, Tasmania, 1988.

Patricia Chalcraft
born 1923

Three-year-old Patricia Chalcraft emigrated to Australia from Wales with her parents and younger sister in 1926. The family settled in Heidelberg, Melbourne, where her father was employed by the Shell Company. He lost his job when the economic depression began to hit Australia in 1928. Desperate to make ends meet, her parents became involved in the Heidelberg Unemployed Bureau. Its weekly meetings at Barkly Hall assisted those out of work to find a range of odd jobs.

They had a fancy dress party and my father wanted to win a prize to buy us shoes. It must have been my father's idea and my mother went along with it. My mother made this dress out of an old curtain and my dad collected all the old paints and painted it to describe what was needed in the way of work. He'd put a lot of effort into the dress. My father spent a lot of nights doing the painting. It didn't cost my father anything, only his time. All the paint was donated, leftovers, exterior paint. The images were selected from people in much the same position as we were, looking for some sort of work. The whole thing is around the types of work the unemployed could do, if it was available.

The dress was my father's hope not only for himself but for all his friends and people that were needing work. If he could in some way help others as well as himself, it was all he wanted. I think by painting this dress he was more or less putting himself in the place of all of these jobs, thinking that he could do it or someone close by could do them, and hopefully that somebody might see it as an advertisement to work if they needed it.

THE CHALCRAFT FAMILY
National Museum of Australia

PATRICIA CHALCRAFT'S FANCY DRESS,
NATIONAL MUSEUM OF AUSTRALIA
George Serras, National Museum of Australia

What I wore on my head was made of cardboard. It was a board with this little figure in black tights. He was in a running position with a sign — 'Have you got an odd job for Daddy?'

My father had hoped that if I did win anything — which it did, the most original [costume] — that we might get a cheque that he might be able to buy a pair of shoes for me, but unfortunately it was a cheque to be used at the newsagent — which bought a book. He let me have the book because he was very disgusted at what had happened. After all his hard work he wanted something more. He was disappointed. He'd put a lot of time into it.

I think it must have been a bit of a false hope. I think it did a lot of good for dad doing it but I don't think many got work out of it because there still wasn't work there. But it did bring people together that were in those circumstances. That's the one thing it did do.

PATRICIA CHALCRAFT, 1999

SOURCES AND FURTHER READING: Patricia Chalcraft, interview with Marion Stell and Sophie Jensen, 21 May 1999, National Museum of Australia.

PETER WOOD
Gavin Souter

Peter Wood
born 1945

Not everyone has viewed Australia as the promised land. Peter Wood's grandparents carried with them a pair of binoculars to sight New Australia in Paraguay in the 1890s. Peter Wood brought the binoculars back to his new country when he migrated to Australia in 1966.

I am a descendant of William and Lillian Wood who were a part of that remarkable group of socialists, bushmen and shearers who left this country in the 1890s to join William Lane in his quest to establish a New Australia in Paraguay.

My grandfather William or Billy as he was always called was the secretary of the shearers union during the famous strikes of 1891. And he was a strong supporter of William Lane.

I think their idealism was too shallow. William Lane had two silly rules. No integration with the local Paraguayans and no alcohol. Of course expecting bushmen not to drink or mix with girls was ridiculous and the experiment was over by 1908.

They all would have liked to have come back to Australia but pride and lack of money meant that my grandparents stayed there.

The future wasn't terribly bright. I feel that there were better opportunities elsewhere.

I came to Australia in 1966. I didn't speak English at the time but I always felt an affinity with Australia.

I was the first of the New Australian descendants to come back and make a new life in Australia. A number of others have followed. We all have done pretty well.

I guess it is ironic that my grandparents left Australia and went all the way to Paraguay to find utopia and didn't find it while I left Paraguay and came back to Australia and found a good life. They were hoping to create a better way of life.

PETER WOOD, 1997

COLONISTS AT COSME, PARAGUAY, 1896
Image Library, State Library of New South Wales

BINOCULARS TAKEN TO PARAGUAY BY PETER WOOD'S GRANDPARENTS, PETER WOOD
George Serras, National Museum of Australia

SOURCES AND FURTHER READING: Peter Wood, 'The promised land', *Australian Story*, ABC TV, Brisbane, 1 November 1997;
Gavin Souter, *A Peculiar People: William Lane's Australian Utopians in Paraguay*, University of Queensland Press, St Lucia, Qld, 1991 (1968);
Anne Whitehead, *Paradise Mislaid: In Search of the Australian Tribe in Paraguay*, University of Queensland Press, St Lucia, Qld, 1997.

He thrust his joy against the weight of the sea,
climbed through, slid under those long banks of foam—

JUDITH WRIGHT, 1946

'LAND, land!' the joyful cry at last,
Long watch and lonely waiting past:
What home-tied heart can understand
Our joy-burst at that cry of 'Land!'

HENRY PARKES, 1885

First I was in raptures with
the beautiful landscape over
the water; then I was sad to
remember it wasn't home;
then I fell in love with that
pretty yellow tree and with
all the flowers — in fact with
everything; and then, one of
the prisoner-servants came
in, and all my joy went in a
moment. I hate seeing
people miserable.

CAROLINE LEAKEY, 1900

After dinner a small breeze sprung up and
to our great Joy we discovered an opening
into the land and stood in for it in great
hopes of finding a harbour.

SIR JOSEPH BANKS, 1770

Will you look at us by the river! The whole restless mob of us on spread
blankets in the dreamy briny sunshine skylarking and chiacking about for
one day, one clear, clean, sweet day in a good world in the midst of our living.

TIM WINTON, 1991

Seeing his scar, the Old Nurse
identifies the bedraggled stranger as
the lost Odysseus. Joy: the recovery of
the near-gone, the given-up-for-dead.
We weep (for joy!) when our happiness
is occasioned by the memory of grief.

SUNEETA PERES DA COSTA, 2000

The ego, bored with its
    self-investigations,
Spreads itself out so thin it
    can fit across
the sea's surface, each
    pocket a glitter for a god.

SUSAN HAMPTON, 1998

Joy

Joy, delight and glee — sheer fun — cheers the heart. To live fully, we should be free to follow our own ideas of joyful existence. The simplest pleasures, shared joys or extreme gladness, can transport us into other worlds. There, hearts thump, happiness reigns, ecstasy is contagious and laughter is free. What a lark!

Francesca Rendle-Short, 2000

People should be free to follow their own ideas of joyful existence, but not to deprive others of their opportunity to what they conceive as a joyful existence.

Roy Wright, 1983

Sweet odours from the aromatic bush filled the air, and every living creature made what noise it could, to show its joy in being happy and free in the beautiful Bush.

Ethel C Pedley, 1906

Our greatest joy to mark an outline truly
And know the piece of earth on which we stand.

Chris Wallace-Crabbe, 1963

Living is thirst for joy;
That is what art rehearses.

James McAuley, 1956

By me sowl I've sat and watched him till
    me heart wid joy would thump,
Just to see the saucy darlin' hook 'em off
    the middle stump.

Guy Eden on Victor Trumper, c.1900

GEEKGIRL®
On loan from geekgirl®

Proud to Boot, 1997, by Imogen Ashlee,
on loan from geekgirl®

generally I am regarded as the original geekgirl. Not because I have been into computers THAT long, but because I coined and popularized the name from 1994. Since I have had so many copycats hanging from my coat tails, I also made a point of having the name trademarked in Australia and other countries. If you ask me what is Rosie Cross. Well, I am a rather quirky 41 year old, who adores the Internet and has a fondness for machines, particularly computers. This passion is rivaled only by my love of dogs and other critters. I get a true sense of joy every morning when I log on to the Internet and every afternoon when I take the dogs to the park.

For people who know geekgirl the online zine (my alter polymediaistic ego) — it is touted as 'the world's first cyberfeminist hyperzine'.

Sydney, 1994 — there were three of us driving in a car one day. Myself, Lisa Pears and my then boyfriend Rob Joyner Jnr. were raving about what we could do on the 'net to blow people's socks off! The web was fresh, wild & wacky. Lisa and I had been thinking of doing a paper zine for a bit, but with the arrival of the web we thought heh let's do both!! Lisa and I wanted to manufacture a zine that was intelligent, witty and feminist. We all tossed around silly names, acronyms etc and then I said I will use my online nick/handle — geekgirl.

I utilised my journo skills, and started to organise geekgirl as a business, selling merchandise, consulting etc. My stock in trade is — audacity, intelligence, vitriol and being pretty cool. I amass information & contacts the way some people cook with sherry!

Grrrls need modems, and glitter and glue. They need to paste up and express themselves. Modems not only connect grrrls with the world, modems are a conduit for self empowerment. A bricolage for the 90s, modems and grrrls go-together like punk and safety pins. And yes, I am post punk and more funk. Put down that pony, and pick up a computer was our first motto in 1994.

When I look into the cauldron of net brew-ha-ha: I ignore the commercial crud and see the magic of DIY and personal expression. It's joyfull now because it was so hard in the beginning. I suffered terribly for being a grrrl on the 'net in the early 90s. I wasn't only a grrrl but a feminist to boot!

If you're not paranoid you can en-joy the internet in such a way it will e-luminate your life with mystery and magic.

Rosie Cross, 1999

geekgirl's first computer, Rosie Cross
George Serras, National Museum of Australia

SOURCES AND FURTHER READING: http://gkgirl.com.au/; Rosie Cross, email interview with Sophie Jensen, 1999, National Museum of Australia.

GWEN MEREDITH
On loan from Gwen Meredith

In 1944 radio writer Gwen Meredith was commissioned by the ABC to write a serial based on people in rural areas during the war; it was called *The Lawsons*. After it had run for five years, Gwen Meredith developed another serial on rural Australia with new characters — *Blue Hills*. It ran for 5,795 episodes, finally finishing on 30 September 1976. Its authenticity enthralled rural Australia.

I thought I must get a name that it doesn't matter where I take this story anywhere in Australia it will be typical, and I thought what is typical of the whole of Australia? Blue Hills — which are everywhere, wherever you go, somewhere you'll see hills blue in the background.

We had drama, certainly, but I've always tried also to have some comedy, I don't mean slapstick, even we've had a bit of slapstick too, but humour. I think this is most essential. I think people want to laugh.

I've never written anything in long hand, no, I started off typing them and I'm a very bad typist, I always have been, I've never learnt to type. This was a very tedious trying business and after about two years, I think it was only two years, I started to use a dictating machine. And I've dictated every episode since.

GWEN MEREDITH DICTATING AN EPISODE OF *BLUE HILLS*
ABC Document Archives

Always if I was doing an American accent I would do it a little American because in this way you can't go wrong with the lilt and the accent and this is why I think dictating is by far the best way of writing dialogue because you simply can't say something that's wrong.

GWEN MEREDITH, 1976

During the life of the serial, Gwen Meredith received thousands of fan letters from all over Australia.

I cannot resist writing to express the immeasurable joy you have given me over long years.

FAN LETTER, 1975

It must be a great sense of satisfaction to know that you have spread so much joy. It's such a clever story, all your characters are so real — so human. And yet you have a terrific ability for not letting them do the expected. We will often say 'wonder what Gwen Meredith will do about this'? But it never quite works out in the obvious way.

FAN LETTER, 1973

I write as a 'Middle aged country cocky' to say thankyou very much for the pleasure you have given me and my family at 6 mins past one each week day for the last 30 years.

FAN LETTER, 1976

I think, there can be few people who have given so much pleasure to so many people.

FAN LETTER, 1964

RECORDING THE FINAL EPISPODE OF *BLUE HILLS*
ABC Document Archives

SOURCES AND FURTHER READING: Gwen Meredith, interview with Tim Bowden, *Blue Hills Revisited*, ABC Radio, Sydney, 1976; Gwen Meredith Papers, MS 6789, National Library of Australia.

HEATHER ROSE
Matt Nettheim

Heather Rose
born 1966

Heather Rose's film, *Dance Me to My Song*, was an official selection in competition at the Cannes Film Festival in 1998. She co-wrote and starred in the film, about a woman with cerebral palsy caught up in a love triangle. A documentary film was made about her journey to Cannes. She wore a gold evening gown to the screening.

HEATHER ROSE IN HER GOLD DRESS AT CANNES, HEATHER ROSE

My name is Heather Rose. I am 32 years old. I cannot walk or talk or wash myself or dress myself or even feed myself. I am completely dependent on other people for everything to do with my living.

When I was 13 I was in a short demonstration film. It had a big impact on me. It was the first time I had seen any filmmaking. It's rare for someone like me to get an opportunity. But I was asked to be in a movie called Bad Boy Bubby *— I liked the script so I agreed.*

When I saw myself projected onto that big screen for the first time I couldn't believe it. I felt like I was part of something. I wanted to learn more. I was hooked but I didn't know where to go.

Sometime after I was communicating with a man named Fred on common ground — a computer-based bulletin board for people with disabilities. Fred had chronic fatigue syndrome. But we discovered we had more in common than just our disabilities. We had both worked on Bad Boy Bubby. *It was too good a chance to miss. I asked Fred if he would help me write a script for a film. He agreed and we embarked on the first draft of our script.*

We called our script 'Dance Me to My Song' and with the involvement of Rolf [de Heer], who directed Bad Boy Bubby, *the film suddenly become a reality. With me in the lead role. It was unbelievable.*

For five weeks my home was taken over by the film production. It was a crazy time. I was more tired than I had ever been. But I wanted to prove I was as good as everyone else.

I feel beautiful not boring and plain. I feel like a star.

Word came back to me that ... the Cannes Film Festival wanted to see the film.

As I watch people doing things for me for my trip to Cannes I think about being dependent. The thought that in some way we are all dependent on others delights me. When you look at it like that I may not be so different at all.

For the first time in my life I am not a burden on society but am making a contribution to it. That is probably the greatest of all feelings I can have. I have grown personally, professionally and even if the film is rejected here today a weight has been lifted from me. I know now I am good enough.

Up the red carpet — towards that cinema with 2,500 people from all over the world in it. All here to watch my film, to judge it, to see if it is good enough to be up there with the best.

As the end credits role we go back inside. The cinema is still full, people are standing, people are crying, people are clapping and cheering. I feel shocked. I want to cry — I am proud — I am happy — I am joyous. I will never forget this not for the rest of my life.

HEATHER ROSE, 1998

Matt Nettheim

SOURCES AND FURTHER READING: *Heather Rose Goes to Cannes*, betacam, 1998, SBS Independent, directed by Christopher Corin, produced by Julie Ryan.

Roy Rene as Mo
Performing Arts Museum, Victorian Arts Centre

Roy Rene —Mo — is regarded by many as Australia's greatest stage comedian. In 1916 he teamed up with Neil Phillips to form the successful Stiffy and Mo duo. He published his memoirs in 1945.

ROY RENE APPLYING HIS MAKE-UP FOR MO, WATCHED BY HIS SON
Performing Arts Museum, Victorian Arts Centre

My stage career started in the back-yard when I was a school boy of about eight or nine, attending the Dominican Convent. With the other kids, I used to run a circus or penny concert every Saturday afternoon ... I used to put on a pretty good show. I dyed my father's underpants black for tights, and I and a pal used to ride a couple of ponies as a bare-back act ... My special piece of business in the show was a lion-tamer's act. I went around the neighbourhood and collected a lot of stray cats and got them in a wire cage. What with me and my tights, it used to go over big.

Now timing was one of the most important things in building up an act. You don't force your audience to laugh, you just wait until they're ready and then you punch the line home.

Nowadays, times have changed, the talkies have introduced a different mood into the theatre itself. They want something snappy and quick ... What you've got to remember is that every night the audience is different.

What is good comedy for one city isn't accepted in another. You have to feel the pulse of an audience and try to give them what they want, but above all you must give them good stuff.

Vaudeville is full of life ... Weekly changes and ad-libbing gave you ideas. It kept you on your toes. Believe me, you had to have ideas, too. With the Stiffy and Mo revue, we only had a couple of hours every morning to rehearse, and we had to get eight new gags every week. And where did we get our gags? From the life all around us, that's where we got our humour, and that's why people came to see us week after week for sixteen years.

We wanted to make our audience laugh, and we went about it the best way we knew.

Ken Hall and Stuart Doyle signed me up to do 'Strike Me Lucky', and I had no hesitation about taking it on. But I only made one picture. I found it too hard trying to be funny to no one ... It was the hardest work I have ever done ... No, really, the truth is, there's one thing I love, and that's my audience, and I am not happy far away from the vaudeville stage, which is where I feel I belong.

ROY RENE, 1945

STATUETTE OF ROY RENE PERFORMING ARTS MUSEUM, VICTORIAN ARTS CENTRE
George Serras, National Museum of Australia

Roy Rene, *Mo's Memoirs: Roy Rene*, Reed and Harris, Melbourne, 1945.

THE WIGGLES
The Wiggles Touring Pty Ltd

The Wiggles
formed 1991

What is Red, Yellow, Blue and Purple and is a lot of fun? It's The Wiggles!

Anthony Field, Murray Cook and Greg Page met while studying Early Childhood Education at Sydney's Macquarie University. The three began writing children's songs as one of their music projects. They enlisted the assistance of Jeff Fatt, who played with Anthony in the popular 1980s band The Cockroaches, and The Wiggles were born.

Greg — *Not all of my magic tricks work, but they are lots of fun!*
Anthony — *Oh food, food, food! I love to eat. Dancing and singing with The Wiggles makes me very hungry.*
Murray — *I have lots of different guitars and I use them all when we record The Wiggles' albums.*
Jeff — *I use up so much energy singing, dancing and having fun with The Wiggles that I need lots of sleep.*

THE WIGGLES IN THEIR COLOURED SKIVVIES
The Wiggles Touring Pty Ltd

TOOT TOOT, CHUGGA CHUGGA, BIG RED CAR

Toot toot, chugga chugga, Big Red Car
We'll travel near and we'll travel far
Toot toot, chugga chugga, Big Red Car
We're gonna ride the whole day long
Murray's in the back seat
Playing his guitar
Murray's in the back seat
Of the Big Red Car
Jeff is fast asleep
He's having a little rest
We'd better wake him up
So let's all call out 'Wake Up Jeff!'
Anthony is eating
He's got so much food
He's eating apples and oranges
And fruit salad too
Greg is doing the driving
He's singing 'scooby-doo-ah'
Greg is doing the driving
Of the Big Red Car
Toot toot, chugga chugga, Big Red Car
We'll travel near and we'll travel far
Toot toot, chugga chugga, Big Red Car
We're gonna ride the whole day long

THE WIGGLES IN THE BIG RED CAR
The Wiggles Touring Pty Ltd

SOURCES AND FURTHER READING: http://www.thewiggles.com.au/; The Wiggles, 'Toot Toot, Chugga Chugga, Big Red Car', *Toot Toot* (CD), 1998.

at night those little squares of yellow light,
so significant in the wide country darkness,
are scattered far and wide like lonely stars.

M. BARNARD ELDERSHAW, 1939

We meet and part now all over the world.
We, the lost company,
take hands together in the night, forget
the night in our brief happiness, silently.
We who sought many things, throw all away
for this one thing, one only,
remembering that ain the narrow grave
we shall be lonely.

JUDITH WRIGHT, 1946

The ABC of Loneliness
apologise   absolute   authorisation / annihilation
crying   cold   calculated / concentration-camp
black   bored   bald / bigotry

JACKIE HUGGINS, 2000

The air's lonelier after the
train noises die. The night
shift at the Roadhouse is the
sad shift. The sound of the
swings outside in the empty
picnic area gives me the
shivers. A terrible loneliness
turns my insides cold.

GILLIAN MEARS, 1997

Alone. An inner emptiness circling
in hope of contact. One degree off zero.
Touched by a light and chilling finger.
The solitary person, forgetting the
forgotten world, moves among others,
cautiously protective of the fragile
pleasure of maturity.

RODNEY HALL, 2000

loneliness

Loneliness can spread a thick desolation.
Out the back of beyond or beneath neon lights
in a city street, you can experience the emptiness
of being alone.
Sense the vastness of this land, feel the solitude.
Loneliness drives people apart or it draws them
together in surprising ways.

FRANCESCA RENDLE-SHORT, 2000

All over the city there are
lonely women leading their
own queer lives, starving
quietly and decently, or
timorously clinging to
some job or other.

KYLIE TENNANT, 1943

Those who live alone in rooms
are perhaps lucky in this
that there as they open the door
in or out to loneliness
there is no lover or child to run
forward quickly, enclosing them
    with otherness.
Here sometimes they pause upon clarity:
I am here and to this I am this.

BARRETT REID, 1995

But the dweller in the wilderness acknowledges the
subtle charm of this fantastic land of monstrosities.
He becomes familiar with the beauty of loneliness.

MARCUS CLARKE, 1896

JACK CASTRISSION
On loan from Peter Castrission

Jack Castrission
1908–1987

Gundagai is regarded as halfway between Sydney and Melbourne on the Hume Highway. The Niagara Café in the main street was run by a family of Greek–Australians. It was the focal point for the rural community as well as passing travellers. Jack Castrission arrived in Australia in 1921, and went straight to Gundagai where his brother and uncle ran the Niagara Café. After travelling, he returned in 1934 to work in the café until his retirement in 1983.

His son Peter reminisced:

THE NIAGARA CAFÉ
On loan from Peter Castrission

The mandolin was his own connection to his beloved Kythera. He played old Kytherian songs on it. It was also a connection to the past and the times he spent with his brothers in Gundagai and the memories of the 'glory days' of the Niagara Café when it was considered the best café in Australia.

The Niagara Café was dad's life. It meant everything to him. He just loved the place, even when he was over 70 years and sick, he still worked there because it gave him pleasure to see people enjoying a good, wholesome, inexpensive meal. He was proud of the traditions the café had, its goodwill and reputation as one of the finest eating establishments on the Hume Highway. He ensured its longevity. He was a shrewd businessman; he was clever in advertising and promotion.

For Gundagai people the Niagara was the centre of the main street. It was a meeting place. After the movies on a Friday and Saturday night in the 1960's you couldn't get a seat. Best thick shakes in the Riverina, jukebox blaring and a series of red, hotted up FJ Holdens parked out the front — real cool!

The café offered fine food, silver service, with waitresses in neat uniforms, espresso coffee or hot chocolate. For the workers mid week it was a place to have lunch. On the weekends it was a place to bring the family for dinner. After Sunday mass at 6pm, many of the farmers would attend mass and then take the family to the Niagara for their weekly treat, a big, juicy rump steak, chips, eggs, grilled tomato and Worstershire sauce all over it! The café was a stopover for the Pioneer express buses. The café could seat over 100 persons and it was not uncommon to have 2–3 buses for lunch, daily in the holiday season. The café was a meeting place for teenagers before and after movies, dances, football matches, anything else that was on.

Dad never forgot his childhood, he had an excellent memory, even though he had left the island in 1921. He was very proud of his Greek heritage. He told us many stories about Kythera when we were young. He described his house, the landscape, the blue clear water.

PETER CASTRISSION, 2000

JACK CASTRISSION'S MANDOLIN,
PETER CASTRISSION
George Serras, National Museum of Australia

SOURCES AND FURTHER READING: Peter Castrission, email interview with Allison Cadzow, 5 May 2000, National Museum of Australia.

LIEUTENANT JANE MCLEAN
On loan from Professor Bob Gollan

Jane McLean
1875–1950

Gold — bright, glittering gold! Brave young women in the Salvation Army went out in small groups across the country to live on the isolated goldfields in the hope of converting miners to God. Typhoid fever was rampant on many goldfields and the 'lasses', as they were called, often nursed the sick as well as holding prayer meetings. They slept on hard stretchers, without sheets, pillowslips, or any 'comforts', surrounded by dangers 'seen and unseen'. Lieutenant Jane McLean travelled with two women to Cue, Western Australia, in 1896. The following reports of their work were published in the Salvation Army newspaper the *War Cry*.

JANE McLEAN (LEFT)
On loan from Professor Bob Gollan

At last the coach pulled up, and the first question we heard was: 'Have the lasses come?' Then one man put his head in through the window, and when he saw us he called out: 'Yes, here they are: three cheers for the lasses!' and three hearty cheers were given, which made us feel we were really welcome. We have come believing for a very blessed term in Cue, so you will hear from us again some future time. God is leading us, and we are in for victory.

Seeing that we folks in Cue are in such a remote part of the world, we think the Cry readers will be glad to hear from us, and we are glad to have good news to tell. On Sunday night the barracks was packed with men — not one woman to be seen but ourselves, who numbered three. They sat and drank in every word that was spoken, and sang till one would almost think the heavens were opened, and the angels could be heard.

JANE McLEAN, 1896

This poem by Minnie L Rowell was published in the *War Cry* in 1896.

'God's Lasses'
Many a lad from homes of love
Over the goldfields daily rove;
Many a lad in his tent has died,
No loving mother by his side.
On to the fields our lasses brave,
Nursing and preaching, have gone to save,
Prodigal boys have come to God,
Many a sick one has been restored,
And the men all round the goldfields say:
'Thank God that the lasses came our way.'
Fever is cruel, and passed not by
Our lasses and even now some lie,
Wasted and ill, in their canvas home,
Wond'ring, when conscious, 'Will Jesus come?'

MINNIE L ROWELL, 1896

SALVATION ARMY BONNET, SALVATION ARMY HERITAGE CENTRE, SYDNEY
George Serras, National Museum of Australia

SOURCES AND FURTHER READING: *War Cry*, 25 January 1896; Minnie L Rowell, 'God's Lasses', *War Cry*, 25 April 1896.

MINETTA HUPPATZ
National Museum of Australia

Minetta Huppatz
1915–1987

As a competition for readers in 1932, the *Adelaide Chronicle* published the pattern for a Farm Life Quilt in weekly instalments. Sixteen-year-old Minetta Huppatz, on an isolated farm in Eurelia, South Australia, won the junior prize for best quilt. She wrote to the newspaper:

I live on a farm, and our nearest town and post office is eight miles away. We get our mail twice a week. We are also 200 miles from the city ... I wish to thank all those readers who have so kindly sent congratulations to me on winning the prize for the Farm Life quilt in the under 18 years competition. I was at the Adelaide Show and saw them all. Mine was done in darning stitch, so you can all guess I had plenty to do for the five months the competition was on.

MINNETA HUPPATZ, 1932

A sense of community was created through the women's pages of the *Adelaide Chronicle*. Rural women felt connected to each other by the threads of the quilt.

MINETTA HUPPATZ AND HER PRIZE-WINNING QUILT
National Museum of Australia

A year ago my 'Digger' husband lost home and everything, owing to the drought, so since then I have had to keep my four children, and ourselves with what I can get for the cream from my three cows ... I rarely go anywhere, as I have taken nearly all my own clothes and made up for my little ones to keep them tidy for school ... I would love to see the Farm Life Quilt section at the Show, but no such luck for me (it is over five years since I had a holiday), so we shall be waiting to hear all about them ...

LETTER, 1932

I am looking forward with great interest to the quilt patterns, and hope to be able to make one, as I am very fond of needlework and do all our sewing and mending. It's mend, mend, mend, mend these times, until there is little of the original article left; yet somehow I feel rather proud of a well mended garment.

LETTER, 1932

We now live nearer a small country town, and are by no means 'outback'. But as we have no car, no music, no electric light, and no telephone, it almost sounds 'outback'. We are lucky enough to have the water laid on ... Often when I am stitching away at the quilt, I wonder how many more girls and women, perhaps hundreds of miles away from each other are working away at the same pattern.

LETTER, 1933

I am 18 years old, and live on a farm about 20 miles from the nearest town. Mother has been very busy making a farm life quilt. She has spent many evenings and afternoons working at it. We had to go in to town every Friday to get 'The Chronicle', and the cotton. Mother would lose practically a night's sleep if these could not be obtained that day. We do not know what we are going to do with her now the quilt is completed!

LETTER, 1932

MINETTA HUPPATZ'S FARM LIFE QUILT,
NATIONAL MUSEUM OF AUSTRALIA
Matt Kelso, National Museum of Australia

SOURCES AND FURTHER READING: Minetta Huppatz, letter, *Adelaide Chronicle*, 20 October 1932; Margaret Rolfe, *Patchwork Quilts in Australia*, Greenhouse, Richmond, Vic, 1987 (1990).

NOELLE SANDWITH
National Museum of Australia

Noelle Sandwith
born 1927

An artist's adventure. In 1952 English artist Noelle Sandwith journeyed alone down the legendary Birdsville Track in search of subjects to draw. She travelled over 6,000 kilometres by the mail truck, stopping and drawing the lonely characters and places she encountered. She produced a remarkable collection of sketches and photographs, and a manuscript detailing her adventure.

'Go to Birdsville, then down the Birdsville Track. One man and a dog have been there!'

I had met the Rev. Fred McKay at his headquarters of the Australian Inland Mission. I found he knew of my drawings and had this advice: 'Only one man and a dog! Go to Birdsville, then down the Birdsville Track, if you want something out of the ordinary!' His words kept recurring to me — an invitation to loneliness, utter loneliness, or success for an artist's pencil. It was both an incitement and a temptation, an achievement to which circumstances prompted, and an opportunity to make drawings of the Real Australia in the back-of-beyond. Birdsville, the town of 'one man and a dog', the land 'where the crows fly backwards', sat just north of the border between Queensland and South Australia, on the brink of the Never-Never. Perhaps recklessly, perhaps without adequate forethought, certainly without being put out of countenance by dismal forecasts of failure — the Birdsville Track lured me by its very name!

SKETCH BY NOELLE SANDWITH
National Museum of Australia

Birdsville survived, thinly scattered along an exposed and wind-swept ridge; its seven buildings and a shack starkly bordering Adelaide Street, a flat wide claypan which straggled bleakly for half a mile. This minute settlement of nineteen white folk was the ultimate back-of-beyond. Situated on the edge of 'Never-Never-Land' — the notorious Simpson Desert — a last outpost of civilization.

It was doubtful whether a lonelier pub existed on this planet. In the centre of a vast expanse of sand, so desolate and empty of life as to suggest a lunar landscape, the tall sky the only boundary.

Sergeant V. Barlow kindly agreed to pose. It really was good of him, for apart from police work — his beat covered 200,000 square miles — he held twenty four other official posts. Among the most important were those of Weather Observer, Inspector of Stock, Postmaster, Agent for the Commonwealth Savings Bank, Superintendent of Traffic(!), Inspector of Brands, Receiver of Taxes, River Observer and Authorised Officer for the Destruction of Dingo Scalps.

NOELLE SANDWITH, 1953

NOELLE SANDWITH'S ART PENCILS,
NATIONAL MUSEUM OF AUSTRALIA
George Serras and Gerald Preiss, National Museum of Australia

SOURCES AND FURTHER READING: Noelle Sandwith, unpublished manuscript, Sandwith collection, National Museum of Australia.

NORMIE ROWE
Trevor Dallen/The Fairfax Photo Library

Normie Rowe
born 1947

From 1963 pop singer Normie Rowe enjoyed success on the Australian music charts as a teenage heart-throb. In 1967 he was conscripted and sent to Vietnam for two years of National Service. On his return he felt alienated, a feeling shared by many of his fellow veterans. He joined the Vietnam Veterans Motorcycle Club, helped organise the Welcome Home Parade in 1987 and was present at the opening of the Vietnam Veterans Memorial in Canberra in 1992.

The memorial is a warning to our politicians to never again send Australians overseas to fight unless they have the full and undivided support of the Australian people, and that never again should Australians be sent away to war and then have to wait 25 years to be welcomed home.

NORMIE ROWE, 1992

In 1999 he wrote 'Missing in Action' to reflect the experiences of Vietnam Veterans everywhere.

His eyes told stories all about the fear and sweat and pain
Of the lives of his young mates that politics flushed down the drain
The enemy at home worse than the foe he fought back there
Of honour duty loss and grief they didn't seem to care.

So he went Missing In Action
From the time he got back home
When he got off of that Freedom Bird
He could feel it coming on
Missing In Action
And feeling all alone
Nobody understood, he never thought they ever would.

So he packed his cruiser hit the road to leave it all behind
Headed north went out on highway one to find some peace of mind
Well he felt the anguish fall away
A comfort he'd not known
Since the comfort that he'd felt when he was all those miles from home
Drop the ammo belt
Can clear the gun
Safe to take off the old bush hat
From the pearly gates
Into the safety they called Nui Dat

Now he's been living all alone in the warmth of Capricorn's caress
Not even giving those he cared about a hint of his address
30 years or more have passed and time can heal a lot of fears
So he set his course for places south
And hid away the tears
As he climbed aboard his Harley
Gave a rev, and dropped away the clutch
He wondered how that girl of '69 might have changed that much
When he arrived back in his small hometown and turned into the drive
He saw her running down into his arms
Glad he was still alive

NORMIE ROWE (LEFT) AT THE WELCOME HOME PARADE
Dean McNicoll, *Canberra Times*

VIETNAM VETERAN'S LOGO AND MOTORCYCLE JACKET
George Serras, National Museum of Australia

SOURCES AND FURTHER READING: *Sydney Morning Herald*, 5 October 1992; Normie Rowe, 'Missing in Action',
Patrons: A Tribute to Australian Vietnam Veterans and Their Families, 1999, Both Barrells Music, Western Australia.

And to see or touch satin, nail lacquer, shoe leather is thrilling
  for its own sake—
Shapes, scents, sounds, superficies are divine.

HARRY HOOTON, 1961

A thousand tiny syncopations in the metronomic measure of everyday life; the
unexpected yet still hoped for flickering rush of thrill's pale underbelly.

ANNAMARIE JAGOSE, 2000

There is a lot of thrills to be got out of fishing,
though not much fish.

LENNIE LOWER, 1932.

Electric fingers send the sudden thrill
Through senses unsubservient to the will;

ADA CAMBRIDGE, 1913

It is with a thrill of cruel suspense
that such prisoners first plant
their foot on Tasmanian ground.

CAROLINE LEAKEY, 1900

My decaying lyre
glows green
under the rubbish mounds

O to live dangerously again,
meeting clandestinely in Moore Park
the underground funds tucked up
  between our bras,
the baby's pram stuffed with illegal lit.

DOROTHY HEWETT, 1975

dumped
it lies in wait
for someone's fossicking fingers

what bone-burning tunes
it will play
through that stray hand!

DOROTHY PORTER, 1996

thrill

To get a thrill out of something, you feel it in your body. A throb. A nervous tremor. It can be a thrill of joy, excitement, anticipation. Or you can experience fear thrill through your veins — by living dangerously, flirting with the forbidden and outrageous. Whatever it is — thrilling yourself, causing a thrill — be moved.

FRANCESCA RENDLE-SHORT, 2000

In an Australian scene you have Nature in her grandest aspect and most gigantic proportions; you gaze around, and the heart thrills, because you feel you are nothing when alone with your Maker.

T McCOMBIE, 1845

Ah, that's good, brother. Live dangerously, live dangerously, there aren't enough people in the world who live dangerously.

WILLIAM MORRIS HUGHES, 1940s

In thoughts that thrill me like a tolling bell.

ADA CAMBRIDGE, 1887

And did her frame thrill with rapture? did she bound to his caress? did her lip falter from her grateful emotion? — did she bury his cheek in her raven tresses?

WH CHRISTIE, 1841

DAVID VRETCHKOFF
On loan from David Vretchkoff

David Vretchkoff
born 1965

David Vretchkoff runs Veg Art Airbrushing and lives on the northern Sydney beaches.

DAVID VRETCHKOFF
On loan from David Vretchkoff

My involvement started when I was 12–13 and I was keen to learn how to surf. I have been surfing for around 22 years now and even though I don't surf as much as I used to every time I paddle out I still enjoy it and I feel fresh and relaxed afterwards. I work within the Surfing Industry designing and creating feature pieces of artworks which I airbrush onto surfboards. I've been doing this for 15 years. These pieces can be simple, or they can be mammoth full mural pieces which require an enormous amount of work. I love these intricate designs, the more difficult, the better.

Even before I was involved with the Surf Industry I always liked to have a piece of artwork on my surfboards. It gives a board character.

The Airbrush tool and what it can do was an attraction. Being paid and at the same time being able to perfect my Airbrush was also an attraction. I am lucky to have a job that I love and enjoy which enables me to become a better artist and also enables me to make a good living from my first love which is Art.

My love of the Ocean [inspires my designs]. When you are surfing and you come so close to dolphins, fish, stingrays and other sea creatures you can't but help be inspired. I am a Piscean. I have always lived by the Ocean and I have a passion to paint anything and everything about it.

If you have ever dived or snorkelled any coral island reef and seen the bright colours of the fish and coral, surfed perfect clean waves or saw dolphins playing in their own playground, you would understand the immense thrill of the Ocean and its awesome power. I try to express this in my Artwork.

A lot of people are often impressed with the realism I am able to capture in an underwater scene. They comment on the use of colour and light that give my pictures realism and authenticity.

If I was to give my style a name I would call it 'Marine Art'. It's a modern style in which I portray my love of all things Oceanic. The colour, the movement, the animal life and the immense beauty of the Ocean ad infinitum.

DAVID VRETCHKOFF, 1999

SURFBOARD ARTWORK BY DAVID VRETCHKOFF
George Serras and Gerald Preiss, National Museum of Australia

SOURCES AND FURTHER READING: David Vretchkoff, written interview with Johanna Parker, 9 November 1999, National Museum of Australia.

JOAN RUSSELL
By Peter Read, Deputy Station Leader, Casey, 1990

Joan Russell
born 1946

In 1990 Joan Russell spent a year as Station Leader at Casey Station in Antarctica amidst the most thrilling landscape. Here are some of her reflections the following year.

JOAN RUSSELL IN ANTARCTICA
On loan from Joan Russell

It is probably the most challenging management job I could envisage and it was time for me to take that challenge.

The year as a station leader taxed my skills to their outer limit and then some. The actual growth this opportunity provided me with is immeasurable ... It's a pretty mind blowing experience. It's perhaps the most bizarre job in the world.

There were twenty three men and three women on the station.

One of the major changes in my life as a station leader at Casey was learning to enjoy, ending up with a very positive feeling about myself as a physical recreationer. Yes, I did learn to ski.

I had studiously avoided all forms of physical exertion as do many women my age and it started in the pre-selection period. As soon as I was invited to an interview I joined a gym ... knowing that by the time the representatives of the Antarctic Division actually set eyes on me I would be a new woman and indeed I was.

It changed my life. I'm quite evangelical about this. There's this sort of endurance knitter, long distance shopper, going to the gym ... I found that in physical terms there was nothing I couldn't handle and it was mostly about mental attitude. It has been a revelation to me and I loved it. It changed my life. It actually changed my life ... It's a wonderful thing. That's a gift. That's another gift from Antarctica to me.

It was a sacrifice. I gave up a lot of things. I gave up control of what I ate. I gave up control of the company I kept. I gave up control of the way I dressed. I left my beautiful clothes behind. I gave up my sexuality. I gave up contact with my family and friends. I gave up the affirmation that comes from being well known and loved and admired.

I did a lot of soul searching. I had a lot of time in my head in a different way, in an entirely different way. I had time to deeply examine my core values and beliefs and I can say for the most part I reaffirmed them. I found strengths, sources of strength previously untapped, about survival, about resilience, about belief in myself, about the maintenance of my dignity in adversity. I found new sources of pride. I have come back very proud.

My year as a station leader was one of the most wonderful years of my life. It was not my whole life. I know that for other station leaders it is the pinnacle, the acme of life. It is their life. It was a wonderful sideways excursion on my already wonderful life.

JOAN RUSSELL, 1991

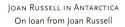

JOAN RUSSELL IN ANTARCTICA
On loan from Joan Russell

SOURCES AND FURTHER READING: Joan Russell, interview with Jill Cassidy, 21 February 1991, Queen Victoria Museum and Art Gallery, Launceston, Tasmania.

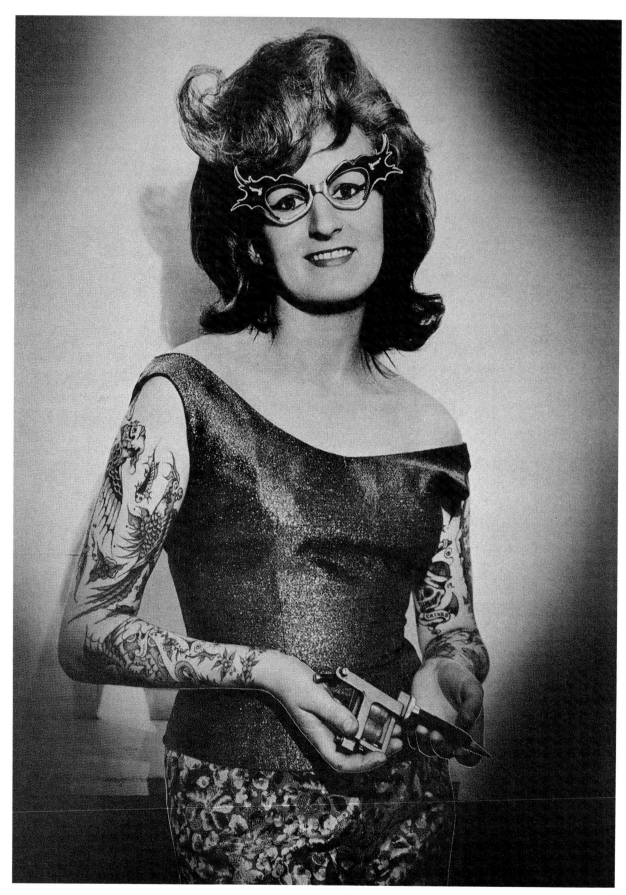

MISS CINDY RAY
Beverley Robinson

Miss Cindy Ray
born 1942

Cindy Ray got her first tattoo on 10 June 1962. She wrote *The Story of a Tattooed Girl* in 1965.

Not long ago I was a very ordinary and very obscure teenager. One day late in teenage life I decided, for the sake of personal adornment, to have a small tattoo put on my back and from this idea developed a whole sequence of events which was to completely change the course of my life.

Today I am solidly tattooed from my wrists to my shoulders, most of my chest, most of my back and both my legs from the knees to my toes are covered with tattooing. I am also an accomplished tattoo artist, I run a tattoo supply business, and in between times I travel the country making public appearances at the larger Agricultural and Royal Shows.

At first I expected to repel the multitudes as an obscene freak, but it has been a great thrill to find that in the majority of cases I have the opposite effect.

MISS CINDY RAY WITH THE TATTOO MACHINE SHE INVENTED
Beverley Robinson

Wherever I go on public exhibition thousands and thousands of people pay their good money and walk into a tent or room for the purpose of looking at me. I am quite sure that a great many of these people think they are coming to inspect some kind of unusual animal on special exhibition for their exclusive benefit, but there is an aspect to this that I am sure they do not realise, and that is that whilst they pay money to look at me I can look at them for nothing, and the criticism is not all one sided.

I can still clearly remember, as I lay on that kitchen table, a feeling in different parts of my back as the linework progressed. At times a sort of burning sensation, at other times just as if the design was being cut in with a knife, and at other times no pain at all.

This is a sensation I have felt many times, when I go to the tattoo studio, knowing that the designs which will be put on my body will be there forever, for the rest of my life.

I have found that tattooing is very much alive today in nearly every walk of life and that some very surprising people, both male and female, are heavily and very secretly tattooed.

When I started to get a reputation for quality work I found that every now and again I would get a request for a really big chest, back or special piece and I must admit that I do get a thrill when I have a chance to do a tattoo piece which gives an opportunity for artistic expression.

MISS CINDY RAY, 1965

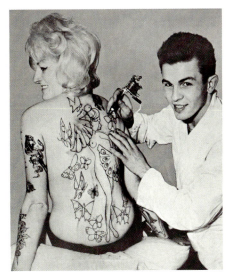

MISS CINDY RAY BEING TATTOOED
Beverley Robinson

SOURCES AND FURTHER READING: Miss Cindy Ray, *The Story of a Tattooed Girl*, self-published, Melbourne, 1965.

REG MOMBASSA
Martina O'Doherty

Reg Mombassa is a Mambo graphic artist. He is a member of the rock band Mental As Anything. He was chosen to design the Australian Olympic uniforms in 2000.

REG MOMBASSA AT WORK
Courtesy Greg Weight

The process of creating something is always thrilling, regardless of whether the work itself is subversive or bland. Finding merit and beauty in the everyday and the commonplace can be thrilling — I call this concept 'the Aristocracy of the normal'.

Sometimes the great spirit of the universe grants a direct but temporary access to that little cupboard in the sky where artistic ideas and images are kept. Other times it's just a matter of looking at the world or at pictures of the world and jumbling, modifying or re-interpreting the images therein.

The concept of thrill is entirely subjective. Some people may be thrilled by my work because of the subject matter or the manner of its execution, while others will be bored or nauseated — it's all in the eye of the beholder.

Drawing pictures for Mambo also provides the opportunity to employ the basest of toilet humours and to make unkind observations about a variety of ideas, individuals and institutions under the guise of decorating some metres of cotton.

Australian Jesus is a local version of the Jesus myth and a useful figure to place in a range of situations both religious and secular. He is also an extension of our interest in national products like Australian wool, Australian music and Australian boot polish. The reverence and informal ritual involved in the use of and handling of much respected everyday objects [inspired this piece]. Australian Jesus looks sad and tired because he is reflecting the fact that most of the lives of most of the people on earth are sad and wearisome, and are only rarely illuminated by moments of joy, peace, relaxation or sexual activity.

REG MOMBASSA, 1999

The Miracle of the Pies and Beer, From the Book of Reg

And it came to pass that Australian Jesus addressed a multitude of 40,000 people at the S.C.G. on his spoken word tour of N.S.W. The day was long and hot, so he said to his assistants they are tired and hungry, give ye them refreshment. And they said unto him, we have but five pies and two cans of warm beer. So Australian Jesus cast his eyes to heaven and began to hand out the pies and beer until all did eat, and were filled. And the beer was cold. It was good.

© MAMBO GRAPHICS P/L '96, REG MOMBASSA

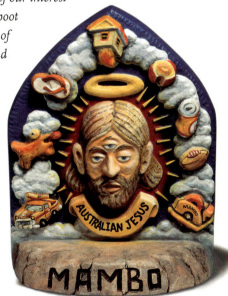

AUSJESUS, REG MOMBASSA
George Serras, National Museum of Australia

SOURCES AND FURTHER READING: Reg Mombassa, written interview, 1999, National Museum of Australia; Reg Mombassa, *Mambo: Art Irritates Life*, Mambo Graphics, Sydney, 1994.

RON MUNCASTER
Penelope Clay, Powerhouse Museum, Sydney

Ron Muncaster
born 1936

Ron Muncaster's spectacular costumes are one of the highlights of the Sydney Gay and Lesbian Mardi Gras. He has won the Best Costume award at Mardi Gras 14 times since the award's inception in 1982. In 1994 he won it for the costume Lucille Balls, which his partner, Jacques Straetmans, wore.

I first entered the Parade in 1980. The first two I watched, thinking 'we can do better than this'. I had a group of friends and we started to make some costumes and floats, headed by Peter Tully who was my hero. I feel very proud that what was started by a handful of people, most of whom are now dead, has become such an international success.

It's amazing how Sydney has taken the Mardi Gras to its heart. I am always overwhelmed when I walk up Oxford Street and reach Taylor Square to hear the cheers from the crowd and see the smiling faces. That's the reward for all the worry and work I put into my costumes.

The work is easy, I love doing it; the worry is that something might break or go wrong. Like the day before the Parade when I had to put the Lucille Balls costume together. It took all day. Then, when my boyfriend Jacques put it on, he said 'I cannot walk in this'. There wasn't enough room in the skirt for him to take proper steps and the balls along its hem kept hitting the ground. He spent that evening practising how to shuffle along.

JACQUES STRAETMANS IN LUCILLE BALLS
Michelle Mika, Photomedia, Sydney

The next day, we loaded a Combi van with cotton blossom and tied the Lucille Balls skirt to the roof. Halfway down William Street, the big skirt fell off the van and held all the traffic up. Not one car beeped their horn, for they saw the plight we were in, and some people got out of their cars to help. Jacques had to sit on top of the van and hold onto the skirt while we slowly drove to the Parade start.

Back in 1982, I made a Carmen Miranda frock with a very long train. There were no barriers in those days, so the street was littered with beer cans. As I walked along I collected all these beer cans under my skirt and it made the most awful noise. Eventually, some kind gentleman lifted the skirt to let the beer cans out.

I never use ostrich feathers, they look so sad when they are wet, and I have seen some feathered tragedies arrive at the Showground.

I was very flattered to be named Queen of Mardi Gras, but I get embarrassed when people curtsy to me.

RON MUNCASTER, 1999

JACQUES STRAETMANS AND RON MUNCASTER AT HOME
On loan from Ron Muncaster

SOURCES AND FURTHER READING: Ron Muncaster, 'Queen of mardi gras (please don't curtsy)', in Richard Wherrett (ed), *Mardi Gras: True Stories*, Viking/Penguin, Ringwood, 1999; Kirsten Tigals (ed), *Absolutely Mardi Gras: Costume and Design of the Sydney Gay and Lesbian Mardi Gras*, Powerhouse Publishing and Doubleday, Sydney, 1997.

The sense of devotion is at once archaic
and wholesome, unfashionable and deep.
It touches the core of our past selves.
Devotion expresses a devotion to the
natural world and to all that world contains,
or implies.

CHRIS WALLACE-CRABBE, 2000

The religion of Australia
is its standard of living.

LLOYD ROSS, 1932

Loved, you are loved, O England,
And ever that love endures;
But we must have younger visions
And mightier dreams than yours;

HAROLD BEGBIE, c.1900

There are awesome, perhaps preposterous
moments when you seem to own love
uniquely, as no one ever owned it before.

SUE WOOLFE, 1996

It never enters my head to leave the Party,
because I simply cannot imagine life outside it.
Not only have I spent the last twelve years of my
life defending its causes, but it has structured my
whole existence, given it special meaning.
Without the communist party I will be adrift
again, at the mercy of a hostile world, with all my
old fears and inadequacies waiting to destroy me.

DOROTHY HEWETT, 1990

devotion

Devoted to a cause or life's work, you are filled with great love. You feel compelled. You rise to the challenge and make sacrifices beyond duty, unfaltering and constant — with grit — to live with loyalty and passion. Devotion can inspire others.
It can drive a life, be all-consuming.
For some, their devotion becomes their life.

FRANCESCA RENDLE-SHORT, 2000

The inner soul divine,
That thinks of going, is already gone.
When faith and love need bolts upon the door,
Faith is not faith, and love abides no more.

ADA CAMBRIDGE, 1913

Strange that I was given
Thoughts that soar to heaven,
Yet must I sit and keep
Children in their sleep!

MARY GILMORE, 1918

Devotion! When thy name is named,
What matchless visions rise!

MARY HANNAY FOOTT, 1885

BENNY ZABLE
Juno Gemes, National Museum of Australia

Environmental artist Benny Zable became a familiar sight at major environment or anti-nuclear protests anywhere in Australia during the 1980s. He epitomised and promoted non-violent protest which he observed on a trip to the United States in 1979 at the time of a major accident at the infamous Three Mile Island nuclear power plant. Benny Zable reflected on his inspiration, his actions and his startling costume.

In the last 5 years I have been performing a character piece as part of a multi-media banner flag installation throughout Australia; protests, festivals, and other events at selective sites on ACTIONS for peace and a sustainable future. I named that character GREEDOZER AND COMPANY. It has been successful at attracting a great deal of media attention. Since 1970 during the Melbourne Arts Co-op days I have been workshopping ideas at festival venues towards developing a process for presenting to a wide and diverse audience. A form of happening theatre, to reach out and activate the consciousness of a multi racial society the common ground we share, the same air we breathe, the same water we drink; a platform for social and environmental reform.

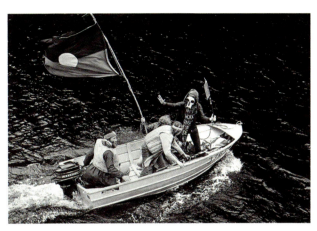

Since the NIMBIN AQUARIUS FESTIVAL in May 1973, it's been an exploration in public art towards inspiring lifestyle changes. Since my journey to the USA in 1979 I have returned to support the PROTEST MOVEMENT. Some of the protests I have contributed to in those days have been Middle Head Sandmining protests action, the Nightcap Rainforest actions, Honeymoon Uranium Mine, Pine Gap USA spy base, Roxby Downs uranium mine, the Franklin Dam blockades, the Nuclear ship actions, and recently the welcoming of the Prime Minister of New Zealand, David Lange, at the New Zealand High Commission, Canberra, for the banning of Nuclear warships from entering N.Z. harbours, making N.Z. a NUCLEAR FREE ZONE.

The beginnings of the GREEDOZER character developed out of a long night of meditation and distress from the forest carnage during the Middle Head sandmining protest actions — October 1980. I visualised a dark character with a skull head, GREEDOZER (death the reaper) image to portray the ugly side of civilization.

GREED + DOZER being two words of multiple meanings

Dozer = bulldozer, asleep, unaware.

BENNY ZABLE, 1984

SOURCES AND FURTHER READING: Benny Zable, Collection no 2, National Museum of Australia.

FAITH BANDLER, 1984
Stuart MacGladrie, The Fairfax Photo Library

devotion

Faith Bandler
born 1918

Faith Bandler was born in the small village of Tumbulgum on the north coast of New South Wales, one of seven brothers and sisters. Her father, a South Sea Islander, was a banana farmer. She played a major role in campaigns on behalf of Aboriginal people in Australia. She detailed these in her 1989 book, *Turning the Tide*.

A great many elements must be present for social change or political change to occur: the time must be right; the society must be made ready; and momentum needs to be built up and maintained. Many people become involved and everyone is touched by the process. In 1967, major political and social change occurred. A referendum was held from which flowed Commonwealth responsibility for Aboriginal affairs, changing forever the social and political relationship between Aborigines and non-Aborigines. The Federal Council for the Advancement of Aborigines and Torres Strait Islanders (FCAATSI) created that change, being itself an instrument created by the changes of the time, yet specifically created to bring about change.

My life became inextricably caught up in FCAATSI — an involvement which on reflection, must have

FAITH BANDLER ON THE BANKS OF THE TWEED, 1999
Patrick Cummins, *Sydney Morning Herald*

been destiny. I was not the only one involved — there were others — but not one of us sought involvement to the extent it occurred. We were bowled over by the power of a social movement which had taken on a life of its own. Totally unprepared for its impact on our lives, we lived, breathed, slept and dreamed its progress, our existence caught up by its existence.

FAITH BANDLER, 1989

Another activist, Dr Roberta Sykes, wrote the introduction to Faith Bandler's book.

I recall first meeting Faith in Townsville, my home town ... It was the first time I'd gone to a luncheon, and I found myself the only black in the otherwise white female audience. I regret I don't recall a thing Faith said as I was so overcome with her poise, dress and charming manner! She wore dainty white gloves and elegant shoes. I had never seen a black woman so elegantly groomed.

I now consider it a put-down to be noticed only for how one is dressed or behaves, and in most instances it is. For me, however, Faith's presentation in Townsville was a mind-boggling occasion. In a flash, all the negative stereotypes of blacks were smashed down ... There was more than just how she looked, however: her careful articulation; her precise use of the English language; and her total presentation which left her audience informed and motivated. I longed to be identified with her.

ROBERTA SYKES, 1987

FAITH BANDLER'S WHITE GLOVES,
NATIONAL MUSEUM OF AUSTRALIA
George Serras, National Museum of Australia

SOURCES AND FURTHER READING: Faith Bandler, *Turning the Tide: A Personal History of the Federal Council for the Advancement of Aborigines and Torres Strait Islanders*, Aboriginal Studies Press, Canberra, 1989.

MARY MACKILLOP
Trustees of the Sisters of St Joseph of the Sacred Heart

78

In 1866 Mary MacKillop co-founded the Sisters of St Joseph of the Sacred Heart (called Josephites), an Australian Catholic order of nuns dedicated to a life of poverty and the service of the poor. After a long campaign by her supporters she was beatified in 1995. She described her life in a series of letters addressed to her family. Here are some extracts.

At last I began to think that my obligations to my family were nearly fulfilled, that others could now take the place I had held, and that I could freely run to God alone.

Long and earnestly as I have wished to enter Religion, the thought of leaving you, my loved Mother, gave me so much pain and anxiety that I had to make it the subject of many Communions.

I longed for a religious life, one in which I could serve God and his poor neglected little ones in poverty and disregard of the world and its fleeting opinions.

Circumstances, as well as choice, having for many years compelled me to live as a teacher, I saw so much of the evils attending a merely secular course of education, that all my desires seemed to centre in a wish to devote myself to poor children and the afflicted poor in some very poor Order.

SISTERS OF ST JOSEPH
Trustees of the Sisters of St Joseph of the Sacred Heart

... I went to open a school at Penola under Father Woods who gradually unfolded to me his idea of endeavouring to do something in the same way for the neglected poor children of South Australia.

From the time I gave myself completely to the work, which almost every day seemed to confirm the vocation I had so long sought, and under the direction of my good Confessor, I found true peace.

I am going to Rome, to the feet of the Holy Father, there to implore his sanction for our holy Rule, and I go full of hope, relying for the success of the undertaking upon the prayers, good observances and charitable dispositions of each and every one of my much loved Sisters.

How little in days past, any of us thought that my duties would take me to Rome to receive a Father's warm blessing and kind encouragement from our Saintly Pontiff; and how little did I ever dream of writing to my sister Annie from London.

Work on with consistency and courage. Bear little trials with patience and love. Remember they all come from the hand of a loving Father and Spouse — and that they are intended to be your stepping stones to heaven ...

MARY MACKILLOP, 1871–1876

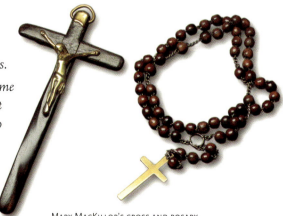

MARY MACKILLOP'S CROSS AND ROSARY,
SISTERS OF ST JOSEPH OF THE SACRED HEART
George Serras, National Museum of Australia

SOURCES AND FURTHER READING: William Modystack, *Blessed Mary MacKillop: A Woman before Her Time*, Lansdowne, Sydney, 1995; Daniel Lyne, *Mary MacKillop: Made in Australia*, Mary MacKillop Secretariat, North Sydney, 1994. Copyright in all quotes is held by Sisters of St Joseph of the Sacred Heart.

ROBYN ARCHER
Robert McFarlane

Robyn Archer
born 1948

A feminist performer, writer and director whose work is known internationally, Robyn Archer is foremost an advocate.

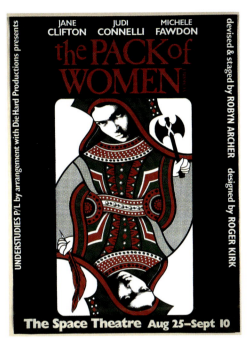

JANE CLIFTON · JUDI CONNELLI · MICHELE FAWDON

the PACK of WOMEN

UNDERSTUDIES P/L by arrangement with Die Hard Productions presents

devised & staged by ROBYN ARCHER · designed by ROGER KIRK

The Space Theatre Aug 25–Sept 10

Image Library, State Library of New South Wales, 1981, copyright Robyn Archer

When I was starting to earn my living from singing there was an idea, certainly in the entertainment world, that anything political was absolute death to a career. Well, I'm political in every possible sense.

ROBYN ARCHER, 1997

I'm protesting at a lot of injustices and just as loud is my protesting at social mores. I think it's very important to express opinions to people right across the board, opinions that they don't exactly agree with.

I was introduced to feminism as one was by women friends in the early 1970s, though I was never part of any group in the women's movement ... I've always lent my support whenever I could ... I've gone on marches, I've sung for tens of thousands of people at Hyde Park in London at one of the big anti-nuclear demos ... Wherever I could, I've always lent my support as an entertainer.

If I was going to be a performer, I was going to be a performer on my terms ... I intended to do thoughtful work, work that came from the heart, work that was an extension of myself. Although many people have tried to foist some title upon me, I've never tried to give a blueprint for any kind of society.

I'm trying to make a statement through my work. I'm talking about things that I find important.

With Pack of Women what I did is put together an entertaining feminist cabaret about women, with lots of features in it by women.

I am pleased with A Star Is Torn ... I really admire all those women as singers ... Politically it really interests me to be able to say those things, because to me it was some kind of resurrection of the dignity of each of those women. And I was very glad about that. But because it used a very popular hook — popular entertainment and popular singers — in both Australia and in London, I got working-class women coming along to that show who were really buzzed by it. The opportunities to do that are very rare.

ROBYN ARCHER, 1987

ROBYN ARCHER'S JUMPER KNITTED BY AN ANONYMOUS FAN, ROBYN ARCHER
George Serras, National Museum of Australia

SOURCES AND FURTHER READING: Robyn Archer in Gloria Frydman (ed), *Protestors*, Collins Dove, Blackburn, 1987; Joanne Tompkins and Julie Holledge (eds), *Performing Women/Performing Feminisms: Interviews with International Women Playwrights*, Australasian Drama Studies Association, Brisbane, 1997.

WILLIAM MORROW
National Museum of Australia

William Morrow
1888–1980

Born in Rockhampton, Bill Morrow emerged as a leader with the Australian Railways Union. He was an active member of the Australian Labor Party and was elected to the federal parliament as a senator representing Tasmania in 1946. The following are extracts from speeches he made to parliament.

I am a product of the trade union movement of this country ... I do not pretend to represent the whole of the people of Tasmania. I shall be quite honest about that. I represent only those individuals who make up the great working class of this country. That class consists of trade unionists, small business men and small farmers. Those people constitute about 95 per cent of the population. The other five per cent consist of those interested in monopolies and combines, and they can be represented by the opposition.

WILLIAM MORROW, 1946

WILLIAM MORROW (IMPERSONATING STALIN)
WITH FRIENDS
National Museum of Australia

If any legislation brought forward cuts across the principles of the people who elected me to this chamber, or would be detrimental to the people as a whole, I shall vigorously oppose its passage. We must not sacrifice our principles merely for the sake of retaining our seats in this chamber, but should make it clear where we stand.

WILLIAM MORROW, 1947

A self-declared international socialist, he devoted his life to world peace. Morrow was awarded the prestigious Lenin Peace Prize in 1961.

The Lenin Peace Prize is the best award a man can hope to win, since it was given to those who take part in the struggle to save humanity.

WILLIAM MORROW, 1961

By a decision of the Committee for the International LENIN Prizes dated 7 April 1961 an International LENIN Prize 'For the Strengthening of Peace Among the Nations' is awarded for outstanding services in the struggle for the preservation and strengthening of peace to William Morrow Australian public leader.

CITATION, LENIN PEACE PRIZE, 1961

Making the most out of the political opportunity Morrow said:

I had to nominate someone from the Prize Committee to present the medal. I asked for it to be on Hiroshima Day and I asked them to send Sahib Singh Sokey. I asked for him because Indians were once British subjects and so more likely to get a visa; he was coloured and that would be a slap at the White Australia policy; and he had more letters after his name than Menzies did.

WILLIAM MORROW, 1961

Dame Mary Gilmore wrote to Bill Morrow with congratulations:

Recognition does matter. It lifts the heart, it gives courage in going on ... You have deserved everything that has been awarded to you — money and recognition. I know no one who has earned it more.

DAME MARY GILMORE, 1961

WILLIAM MORROW'S LENIN PEACE MEDAL,
NATIONAL MUSEUM OF AUSTRALIA
George Serras, National Museum of Australia

SOURCES AND FURTHER READING: Audrey Johnson, *Fly a Rebel Flag: Bill Morrow, 1880–1980*, Penguin, Ringwood, 1986.

It seems as though each man is surrounded by a sphere of known things within which he moves and lives. Beyond this stretches the blackness of the unknown, with its consequent primitive fears and superstitions ... It is fear which kills, fear which paralyses, fear which either prevents constructive action or produces blind panic.

PHILLIP LAW, 1960

Us mob not scare from whiteman, Dagay, no. But it's true—whiteman got no Dreaming for this country. Mebbe he just finish us with his rubbish thinking ... That is a proper scary thing for Aboriginal peoples—to live without a Law. How?

MELISSA LUCASHENKO, MURRI WOMAN FROM BRISBANE, 2000

'Git out,' she replies, though she trembles with fear, For she lives all alone and no neighbours are near; But she says to herself, when she's like to despond, That the boys are at work in the paddock beyond.

HENRY LAWSON, 1912

Everyone is still afraid, or most of us, of this country, and will not say it. We are not yet possessed of understanding.

PATRICK WHITE, 1957

The natives aver that when night comes, from out the bottomless depths of some lagoon the Bunyip rises, and in form like a monstrous sea-calf, drags his loathsome length from out the ooze. From a corner of the silent forest rises a dismal chant, and around a fire, dance natives painted like skeletons. All is fear-inspiring and gloomy.

MARCUS CLARKE, 1896

Fear

Feel fear? Be very afraid.
Perhaps the strongest of all emotions fear can crucify
your body. Faced with impending danger, your hair
stands on end. Blood runs cold. Flesh creeps. Adrenalin
pumps as you flinch, shake or quiver, even petrify.
Terrors by their nature must be faced alone. But in
retelling the horror, fear *can* unite.

Francesca Rendle-Short, 2000

you fall into the circus
of the mind's eye
its breathless desire for flight
as if only feet
hang on like fear
to what is earthed
and deadly with risk

Patricia Sykes, 2000

you try to get out of the fear
by going into it

like quicksand it holds you
like a mother it will not let you
go

Carol Novack, 1974

Diving for fish amongst this weed we learn
sharks and neuroses have that tiger-grin
and all our terrors must be faced alone.

Frank Kellaway, c.1970

GEZA VARASDI
On loan from Dr Geza Varasdi

Geza Varasdi was born in Budapest, Hungary. He was an Olympic athlete. Just before he was due to leave for the Melbourne Olympic Games in 1956, Soviet Union tanks rolled into Hungary and a revolution broke out.

HUNGARIAN ATHLETES ENTER THE OLYMPIC STADIUM,
MELBOURNE 1956
La Trobe Picture Collection, State Library of Victoria

At 14 years of age I had a great urge to run and I went to the sport ground and they welcomed me. This was during the war years and if you were regularly attending then you got a bread roll and a glass of milk after the training program which was fantastic.

In 1952 I was selected for the Olympic team and we got to Helsinki where our team got third place. It was an indescribable feeling. After the Olympic games I continued further and I managed to get into the 1956 Olympic team. Before we were supposed to come to Australia to acclimatise the revolution broke out.

There was a big debate over shall we come or shan't we and eventually the decision was to let us go and to draw the attention of the world to what was going on at home.

Every time we went out to the Western countries there was always some strange people that accompanied us who were disguised as trainers or masseuse or something. But we knew who they were. We had to be very cautious about how we were reacting to things and what we said.

Previously, when we were taken out to Western countries to compete we were always warned that if any of us defected our relatives would be taken to the Concentration camp.

Unfortunately, the tension, the uncertainty, the fear about our families was very great. We really didn't concentrate on the competition as we normally would have done.

Various rumours were floating around but I managed to get a telegram through a friend of mine who escaped Hungary and he sent me a telegram from Vienna saying 'stay — total anarchy — no retaliation' so this reassured me.

I asked one of the Hungarian students who were here earlier, because I couldn't speak a word of English, to take me to the immigration department. This was during the games and they were very friendly to me and they said to me that I can stay here provided I take part in the games that I was brought here for. The 1956 revolution made it possible for me to make this step. I considered myself very lucky.

I was renting a ten by ten foot little bungalow at the back of a house and I was the happiest man. When I put my head on the pillow I didn't have to worry that maybe I had made some wrong expression or wrong remark somewhere and that they would pull me out of bed in the early morning and I'd disappear for ever.

My living standard as a basic wage earner here, as a non English-speaking labourer, was much higher than when I was a doctor behind the iron curtain in the workers paradise.

Hitler and Stalin only differ from each other in colour. They were all based on genocide, fear, terror and poverty. Having experienced five years under Hitler and eleven under Stalin, I think I'm in heaven here.

DR GEZA VARASDI, 1999

GEZA VARASDI'S RUNNING SHOES AND
1956 OLYMPIC GAMES COMMEMORATIVE MEDAL, GEZA VARASDI
George Serras, National Museum of Australia

SOURCES AND FURTHER READING: Geza Varasdi, oral history interview with Sophie Jensen, 28 November 1999, National Museum of Australia.

KIM EASTMAN AND SUSIE AULICH
On loan from Kim Eastman

putting a little life into death

Kim Eastman
born 1956

Susie Aulich
born 1961

Fear

For three years Kim Eastman and Susie Aulich ran a business in Launceston, Tasmania, working with local artists to produce distinctive handcrafted non-traditional coffins and caskets.

We started in 1996 with the concept of bringing a little life into the business of death. We thought that the coffins on offer, all of similar shapes and varying shades of brown, were boring and depressing and expressed nothing of the life of the person inside them. We believed women, as nurturers, could bring a fresh perspective to this male dominated industry.

[The Australian way of death] can be a very 'hands off' affair with a family often forced to make choices at a vulnerable time. Up until recently as a society we have tended to believe death should occur in a hospital situation and funerals should be conducted as sombre, dark ceremonies orchestrated by funeral 'directors'.

A custom coffin is a celebration of a person's life. It makes the statement that the person inside is an individual and not afraid to carry that mark of individuality to the grave. It gets people thinking about death, discussing it with family and friends and begins to break down the barriers which keep us from accepting death as part of life.

It offers people true choice and a say in just how traditional or way-out they wish to be in death. It makes them consider exactly what the loss of this person means and how best to express that. In the case of terminal illness it often allows the family an entrance into the grieving process by a hands on involvement with the coffin theme and its message.

SUSIE AULICH AND A FAUX LEOPARD-SKIN COFFIN
On loan from Kim Eastman

Final Indulgence was started and is run by women. Women seem to have a more rounded and nurturing approach to death. The term Funeral Director is from the male perspective. Whereas today women prefer to be known as facilitators to enable the families involved to direct their own service and to participate fully in the process.

It's about being just as stylish and imaginative in death as you are in life.

KIM EASTMAN AND SUSIE AULICH, 1999

MERMAID COFFIN BY GAYNOR PEATY, NATIONAL MUSEUM OF AUSTRALIA
George Serras, National Museum of Australia

SOURCES AND FURTHER READING: Kim Eastman and Susie Aulich, written interview with Marion Stell, 14 December 1999, National Museum of Australia.

MARY LEE
On loan from Mary Lee

An older generation of Darwin residents have been evacuated at least twice in their lives — once during the Japanese bombing of Darwin in 1942, and again when Cyclone Tracy hit Darwin in 1974. Each evacuation compounds the memories of the other. Evacuees accumulate few treasured possessions.

All I remember was that my mother said that we're going away and we're not to take anything we just have to go. We are only going to Katherine, she said, and it's not far away. She was told only to take a small suitcase for nine of us. The Japanese planes came and it was Uncle Norm who identified them because there was no warning, nothing, and we all ran out to have a look. And we were frightened and my mother was terrified because we could see them, smoke and everything, and the bombs dropping. It was wartime so we ran down the banks of the Katherine River. Uncle Norm made us dig our little trenches and then the bombs fell. I'll never forget. It was terrifying. My mother was just terrified because we had just heard news before that my father was killed during the first bombing of Darwin.

THE LEE FAMILY
On loan from Mary Lee

There was more fear with Cyclone Tracy because I was older, remembering bits and parts of the bombing when I was a child, and knowing what my children were going through with Cyclone Tracy. And no husband. On my own with all these kids. So it was a different feeling, a different fear this time. A really worse fear, I think, for me. I knew who I was, an Aboriginal person and a mother and that, but it was more for my children and I just didn't want anything to happen to them. I was listening to the radio, they said stand in the doorway or go in your little pantry or go in the bathroom. They're the strongest part of the house. So I put all the Christmas presents under the tree. It was a black out. The wind was getting too strong, that was when I started to panic. I didn't know what to do cause still the memories of the war, you see. I was younger then and I thought we'll stand right here in the front lounge and then a piece of wood came through the louvre glass. There was glass everywhere, luckily the kids were covered up. So here am I and I thought if I panic, I'll panic these kids. There was noise, wind, things flying. Oh, I thought, What do I do? What do I do? I was crying, kids were screaming, I'm shaking and then I think, where's my husband, what's happened to him. So we went all in the bathroom, standing room only, cause it's a small bathroom with a bathtub, the noise, and the water was coming through the house. I wouldn't let the kids out of this little bathroom for nearly twenty-four hours ...

I can still hear it, you know, but the crashing noise you just, your imagination, because it's pitch black. You know what that does and what fear does to you, doesn't it? And then I'm thinking now is my husband alive — my father died. Am I a widow? I am thinking all these things, with all these kids.

They said that they were evacuating women and children first to where ever you wanted to go. They had every available plane, Qantas, RAAF, everything. They had everything — but the crush! People were crazy. All traumatised those that weren't injured. They took the injured out first and then they took the mothers and children. So we had to fill in these forms — registration form — so they could keep a track of where all the evacuees went to.

Being older now I would have a fear of dying in another country that is not mine and my spirit wouldn't go back.

MARY LEE, 1999

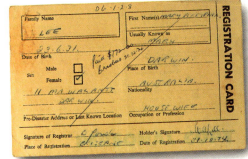

REGISTRATION CARD, MARY LEE
George Serras, National Museum of Australia

SOURCES AND FURTHER READING: Mary Lee, oral history interview with Johanna Parker, 31 August 1999, National Museum of Australia.

VIOLET ROBERTS AND BRUCE ROBERTS
The Fairfax Photo Library

In December 1975 Violet Roberts and her son Bruce Roberts were arrested and later gaoled for killing Violet's husband, Eric. No mitigating circumstances were considered at their trial. Violet received a life sentence and Bruce, a minor, 15 years. The law required that a defence of provocation could only be argued if the killing was done 'in the heat of the moment'. Violet had suffered violence and abuse for over 20 years. In response to this injustice a 'Free Violet and Bruce Roberts Campaign' was organised and a vigil set up outside parliament house in Sydney. The group lobbied at every opportunity. Both men and women identified with the cause and offered generous support. Artist Toni Robertson made a banner that featured regularly on the television news. Violet and Bruce were released in 1980 and the Crimes Act was amended in 1982 to recognise that provocation could build up over a number of years.

A public petition was published in the *Sydney Morning Herald* in October 1980.

We don't want special treatment for Violet and Bruce Roberts — we want justice. It's nearly five years since Violet and Bruce were jailed for the killing of Eric Roberts. Violet and Bruce were the victims of domestic violence. When they sought protection from the police and the courts they got none. Yet, at their trial, there was little evidence given of the history of violence they had both endured. Other women and children in similar cases have been treated more sympathetically — some have been placed on bonds or acquitted — when the courts were made aware of the full facts … We, and the 35,000 people who have signed our petition, call on this government to release them NOW.

TONI ROBERTSON (CENTRE) PAINTING THE BANNER
Virginia Coventry

Violet Roberts made her own plea.

I, Violet Roberts, wish to make application for release on licence … While I certainly do not think there is any good reason to kill anyone, when one suffers so much as my husband caused me to, the savage beatings, the mental torture and sexual miseries … one lived in constant fear of him. My husband was a brutal alcoholic … During those last 12 months, I was seldom without black eyes, bruises … two days before the crime, he had broken a bone in one of my fingers. In addition to all the other troubles, I lost a very dear son, David, just 21 of leukemia … I was so distraught, depressed, so very tired that night, I had not had a good night's sleep for months as every night he kept me awake with his insatiable sexual demands … very little of my husband's behaviour was mentioned in court. I do hope you will look favourably on this, my application. I would certainly abide by whatever restrictions were placed on me, I would just be so happy to be home again.

VIOLET ROBERTS, 1980

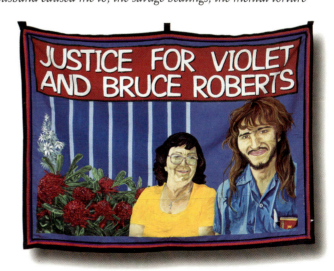

BANNER PAINTED BY TONI ROBERTSON, TONI ROBERTSON
George Serras, National Museum of Australia

SOURCES AND FURTHER READING: Advertisement, 'Release Violet and Bruce Roberts', *Sydney Morning Herald*, 13 October 1980; Violet Roberts, Application for release on licence, 1980, in Robyn Archer, Diana Manson, Helen Mills, Deborah Pary and Robyn Stacey (eds), *The Pack of Women*, Hessian/Penguin, Ringwood, 1986.

ZANE GREY

From Zane Grey, *An American Angler in Australia*, Hodder & Stoughton, London, 1937

94

The American Western writer and big-game fisher Zane Grey came to Australia in 1936 in search of shark. Among the sharks he caught on his trip was a world-record tiger shark 'Length, thirteen feet ten inches. Weight, one thousand and thirty-six pounds' that he caught off Sydney. The following extracts from his book, *An American Angler in Australia*, detail the fight.

ZANE GREY'S WORLD-RECORD CATCH
From Zane Grey, *An American Angler in Australia*,
Hodder & Stoughton, London, 1937

Fifteen minutes later something took hold of my line with a slow irresistible pull. My heart leaped. I could not accept what my eyes beheld. My line slowly payed off the reel. I put my gloved hand over the moving spool in the old habit of being ready to prevent an overrun. Still I did not believe it. But there — the line stripped off slowly, steadily, potently. Strike! There was no doubt of that. And I, who had experienced ten thousand strikes, shook all over with the possibilities of this one.

By now the sport and thrill had been superseded by pangs of toil and a grim reality of battle. It had long ceased to be fun. I was getting whipped and I knew it. I had worked too swiftly. The fish was slowing and it was a question of who would give up first.

The water opened to show the back of an enormous shark. Pearl gray in color, with dark tiger stripes, a huge rounded head and wide flat back, this fish looked incredibly beautiful. I had expected a hideous beast.

The huge tiger rolled over, all white underneath, and he opened a mouth that would have taken a barrel. I saw the rows of white fangs and heard such a snap of jaws that had never before struck my ears. I shuddered at their significance. No wonder men shot and harpooned such vicious brutes!

We towed our prize into the harbor and around to the dock at Watson's Bay, where a large crowd awaited us. They cheered us lustily. They dragged the vast bulk of my shark up on the sand. It required twenty-odd men to move him. He looked marble color in the twilight. But the tiger stripes showed up distinctly. He knocked men right and left with his lashing tail, and he snapped with those terrible jaws. The crowd, however, gave that business end of him a wide berth. I had one good long look at this tiger shark while the men were erecting the tripod; and I accorded him more appalling beauty and horrible significance than all the great fish I had ever caught.

'Well, Mr Man-eater, you will never kill any boy or girl!'
I flung at him.

That was the deep and powerful emotion I felt — the justification of my act — the worthiness of it, and the pride in what it took.

ZANE GREY, 1937

ZANE GREY'S FISHING ROD AND REEL, NATIONAL MUSEUM OF AUSTRALIA
Gerald Preiss, National Museum of Australia

SOURCES AND FURTHER READING: Zane Grey, *An American Angler in Australia*, Hodder and Stoughton, London, 1937.

Crool Forchin's dirty left
'as smote me soul.

CJ DENNIS, 1915

But my languid mood forsook me, when I found a name that took me;
Quite by chance I came across it — 'Come-by-Chance' was what I read;
No location was assigned it, not a thing to help one find it,
Just an N which stood for northward, and the rest was all unsaid.

AB PATERSON, 1891

Australians will buy a raffle ticket in anything. They got into the habit
during the Depression. Buying raffle tickets is like going to church or
drinking beer, once you get into the habit.

FRANK HARDY, 1965

The perfect wisdom of chance:
certainties become fluid and
forgiving, like a river feeling
its way along a body of land.

KATE GRENVILLE, 2000

warming her fingers
over the gas
she types at the kitchen table
Bluey walks the linoleum
whispering *will I kill her
tonight or tomorrow*

DOROTHY HEWETT, 1987

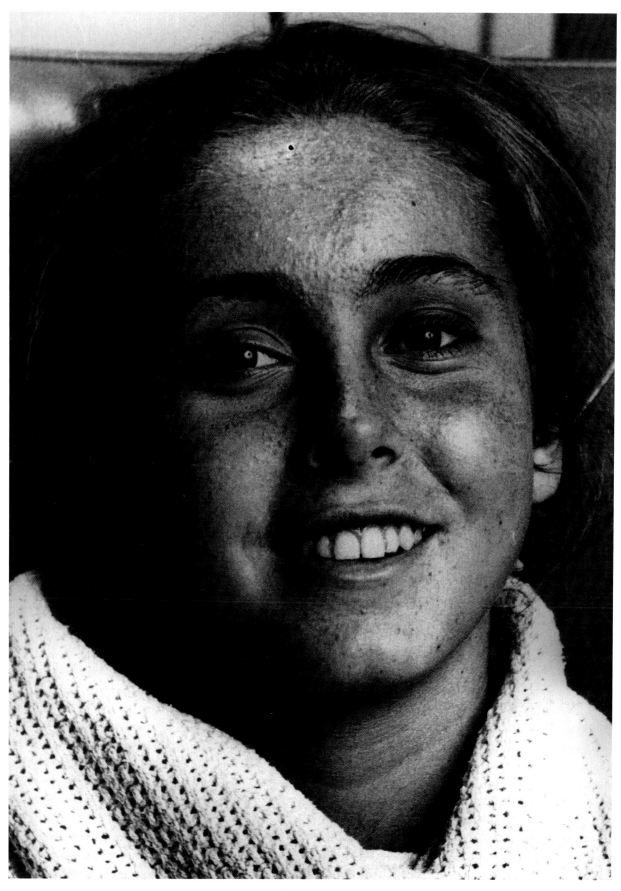

FIONA COOTE
Graham McCarter

CHANCE

A moment in time can change the direction of a life.
For better or for worse. It might be an accident,
a fluke, coincidence, or by taking a risk.
Is it luck? Chance? Fate? A lottery?
Just to be born is said to be lucky.
Life then tosses up possibilities, moments to grasp.
A chance to live *and live* again.

FRANCESCA RENDLE-SHORT, 2000

Love is a gamble,
an' there ain't no certs.

CJ DENNIS, 1915

Strike me lucky!

ROY RENE, 1916

To be born is to be lucky.

KYLIE TENNANT, 1943

Australia is a lucky country
run mainly by second-rate
people who share its luck.

DONALD HORNE, 1964

Australia is a large country with a small
population, far from the rest of the world.
No one goes there by chance, for it is not
on the way to anywhere else.

IAN BEVAN, 1954

JOHN ROSS
Courtesy John Ross, from the WH Ross collection

the luckiest little girl	# Fiona Coote born 1970

Australia's first heart transplant program in 1968 failed to attract public support — the first three patients all died within two months. By the 1980s heart transplant patients had a 52 per cent chance of surviving five years.

On Friday, 30 March 1984, 14-year-old schoolgirl Fiona Coote in Manilla, NSW, felt unwell — but her shortness of breath, weakness and vomiting did not stop her attending school that day. She was determined not to miss the Tamworth Show later that night. But she deteriorated rapidly and was diagnosed with cardiomyopathy, a viral condition that prevents the heart acting as a pump. Doctors at Royal North Shore Hospital in Sydney, where she was quickly transferred, gave the previously healthy teenager only days to live. She needed a heart transplant. Her parents made a nationwide appeal for the donation of a compatible heart.

Her story caught the public imagination, and thousands showed support — some even offered their own hearts. Australia waited. Finally, eight days after she had become ill, a suitable heart was available. The public held its breath on Sunday, 8 April 1984 as Dr Victor Chang led a team of surgeons at St Vincent's Hospital in a four-hour heart transplant operation utilising the new immunosuppressant drug Cyclosporin A.

Four weeks later Australia's youngest person to undergo a heart transplant sent this open letter:

FIONA COOTE WAVES FROM THE BALCONY OF
ST VINCENT'S HOSPITAL, SYDNEY
The Fairfax Photo Library

Thank you Australia

I would just like to let you know how grateful I am and how I realise now that I am the luckiest little girl to have my life.

The other night I felt like giving up. I didn't because of the tremendous amount of support and encouragement given to me by everyone.

Prayers have been said for me. Telegrams, flowers, cards, letters, phone calls and gifts have been sent to me.

The strange thing about all this is that many of these wishes have come from people I don't even know — they were just concerned, loving Australians and that made me feel like not turning back.

I want to say special thanks to the doctors and staff of the Royal North Shore and Saint Vincent's hospitals for giving me my second chance of life — and I feel sure that the Lord is on my side too.

Thank you everyone.

With your help I am going to make it.

God bless you all.

Yours sincerely.

Fiona Coote

St Vincent's Hospital Critical Care Unit.

8 MAY

Fiona Coote was discharged from hospital seven weeks later. She survived the transplant, lung, liver and kidney collapse. Her story had a dramatic impact on the donor program.

STUFFED TOYS SENT TO FIONA COOTE AFTER HER OPERATION,
FIONA COOTE
George Serras, National Museum of Australia

SOURCES AND FURTHER READING: *Sydney Morning Herald*, 9 May 1984.

On or about 19 November 1941, somewhere off Carnarvon on the Western Australian coast, HMAS *Sydney* came upon the German raider *Kormoran*, disguised as a Dutch merchant vessel. In the ensuing action both were sunk. More than 300 of the raider's crew survived in lifeboats or were picked up, and 80 were killed. The *Sydney* disappeared with all 645 hands without a trace. John Ross who had served on the *Sydney* for six years, had been transferred to the *Canberra* weeks before.

THE ILL-FATED OFFICERS FROM HMAS *SYDNEY*
Courtesy John Ross, from the WH Ross collection

As there was time available before my train departure for Sydney, Captain Burnett kindly granted me two weeks' leave to be married and have a honeymoon break before Mollie and I left for that port where Canberra was based, and although it had to be arranged at a most hectic few days' notice we were able to hold the ceremony on 15th October. The Captain and all my messmates not on duty were amongst our guests, and their wedding present to us was an item that is now of great historical as well as sentimental value — a silver salver suitably inscribed and with the specimen signature of every officer engraved on it. Exactly five weeks later and at about the same hour as our wedding every one of these fine men and good friends was lost with the ship.

I find it difficult to describe my feelings of shock and extreme sadness when I knew finally that Sydney and all in her had been destroyed. The English language contains many adjectives — one or more for every occasion — but the nearest I can get is to say that I was, to use the jargon, 'shattered', badly shocked and depressed by the whole matter. It was hard for me to credit that this fine ship and its experienced crew of 645 were gone for ever. My thoughts went firstly to Captain Burnett and all my messmates who had been so happy together at my wedding only five weeks before and then to the members onboard of my Department with whom I had been working so closely and then I thought of the rest of the ship's company — all gone! I knew every one of them in some way or another as one of my duties was to pay them every fortnight and to assist with the keeping of their pay and service records.

It was a national disaster that affected thousands of families spread over every State, in every city and most major towns.

JOHN ROSS, 1994

THE SILVER SALVER PRESENTED TO JOHN ROSS, JOHN ROSS
George Serras, National Museum of Australia

SOURCES AND FURTHER READING: WH (John) Ross, *'Lucky Ross': An R.A.N. Officer 1934–1951*, Hesperian Press, Carlisle, WA, 1994; WH Ross, *Stormy Petrel: The Life Story of HMAS Sydney*, Patersons Printing Press, Perth, WA, 1946.

it can happen to anyone

Kali Wilde
born 1961

KALI WILDE
Peter Gadsden

Thalidomide (alpha-phthalimido-glutarimide) was developed by the West German firm Chemie Grunenthal. It was marketed in Germany from October 1st, 1957 until November 27th, 1961 as a sedative and sleeping pill under the name of Contergan. The firm aggressively advertised thalidomide as safe for pregnant women experiencing morning sickness or trouble sleeping, safe for the foetus, and safe for nursing mothers to use. It was later discovered that thalidomide damages the foetus if taken between the 34th and 50th day after the last menstruation. But by this time thalidomide was available in 75 countries under 73 different names. Approximately 12,000 children were born damaged by thalidomide worldwide. Less than 5000 of us survive as adults today.

Thalidomide can affect the arms, hands, fingers, legs, feet, toes, eyes, ears, noses, nerves, muscles, veins, the heart, the gall bladder, the appendix, the urinary tract (kidneys, ureter, bladder), the genitals and reproductive organs (testis, penis, vagina, fallopian tubes, ovaries, uterus), and the respiratory tract including the lungs, depending on which day in the 17 day window period it is taken. In Australia, thalidomide was available from April 1958 as samples, and sold from June 1960 to December 1961. By June 12 1961, Dr William McBride, a Sydney obstetrician was certain that thalidomide affected the development of the foetus. He alerted Distillers Company Biochemicals (Australia), (the Australian manufacturers) of his suspicions. By early December 1961, thalidomide had been taken off the market in Australia, Great Britain and New Zealand. Thirty-seven Australians are verified as having been affected by Thalidomide. 17 were born in NSW, 8 in Victoria, 6 in Qld, 4 in SA, and 2 in WA.

I established the Thalidomide Network in late 1994 for people affected by thalidomide or who have a similar disability. I did so as many of us affected by thalidomide were experiencing a deterioration in our health, and living with high levels of physical pain. Many parents of children with a similar disability are in contact with the Thalidomide Network, seeking adult role models for their children, and support/information.

Chance fascinates me. I was conceived in Britain during the short time span thalidomide was available. My mother experienced debilitating morning sickness, and was given thalidomide to combat it. She took this drug during the 17 day window period it could damage the foetus. And so, I was born with 2 short arms and kidney damage, and have developed scoliosis and intervertebral fusion as a result of how I have had to use my body to achieve everyday tasks. I moved to Australia in 1973.

I am an artist. Creativity is my passion. I have exhibited my etchings, lino cut prints, and collages in numerous Mardi Gras exhibitions since 1990. My work which addresses both issues of disability and sexuality/sensuality is well known in the gay and lesbian community. I am also a disability activist. I am well known in NSW and the ACT for my work around violence against women with disability, and improving access to support services for these women.

I was given this beautiful Kuan Yin statuette by a friend of mine for my birthday many years ago. It is my most treasured possession. (In Chinese Buddhism, Kuan Yin is the feminine bodhisattva, or Buddha-to-be. She is a symbol of human compassion, peace and generosity.) My friend told me she thought of me when she saw Kuan Yin's many arms. I just cracked up laughing, and fell in love with the statuette. Yep, I have a warped sense of humour!!!

KALI WILDE, 2000

KALI WILDE'S KUAN YIN STATUETTE, KALI WILDE
George Serras, National Museum of Australia

SOURCES AND FURTHER READING: Kali Wilde, email interview with Marion Stell, 2000, National Museum of Australia.

WILLIAM BUCKLEY

Detail: *William Buckley Discovering Himself to Early Settlers*, by OR Campbell, *Illustrated Sydney News*, 24 April 1869, State Library of Victoria

The convict William Buckley escaped in 1803 and spent the next 32 years living as a 'wild man' with the Watournong Aboriginal people near Geelong, before he gave himself up to white settlers. The fortunes of his life have been attributed by many as the origin of the Australian saying 'you've got Buckley's chance'. He could neither read nor write, but others have set down his story using his words.

WILLIAM BUCKLEY
William Buckley Discovering Himself to Early Settlers, by OR Campbell, *Illustrated Sydney News*, 24 April 1869, State Library of Victoria

At the barrack yard I was one day accosted by a woman, who requested me to carry a piece of cloth in a parcel to a soldier's wife in the garrison to be made up ... I took the parcel to do as she wished, and was almost immediately arrested for theft, with the cloth in my possession ... My statement was not believed, and I was sentenced to transportation for life, and sent out in the convict ship ... intended to form a settlement on the southern coast of Australia.

I and two other convicts resolved to escape, proposing to conceal ourselves in the bush until the ship sailed, and then to endeavour to make our way to Sydney, which we thought could not be far distant.

The attempt was little short of madness, for there was before me the chances of being retaken, and probable death, or other dreadful punishment; or again, starvation in an unknown country inhabited by savages, with whose language and habits, I was totally unacquainted, besides the dangers innumerable which the reader may in part imagine, but which no man can describe — no, not even myself; although, by the merciful providence of God, I surmounted them all.

They called me Murrangurk, which I afterwards learnt, was the name of a man formerly belonging to their tribe, who had been buried at the spot where I had found the piece of spear I still carried ... they fancied me to be one of their tribe who had been recently killed in a fight, in which his daughters had been separated also ... To this providential superstition, I was indebted for all the kindnesses afterwards shown to me.

I now made up my mind to continue with the tribe who had received me so kindly, and to accommodate myself to their habits, and, giving up all thoughts of ever seeing my countrymen again, to live as one of them.

I had almost given up all hope of ceasing my savage life, and as man accustoms himself to the most extraordinary changes of climate and circumstances, so I had become a wild inhabitant of the wilderness, almost in reality. It is very wonderful, but not less strange than true. Almost entirely naked, enduring nearly every kind of privation, sleeping on the ground month after month, year after year, and deprived of all the decencies, and comforts of life, still I lived on, only occasionally suffering from temporary indisposition. I look back now mentally to those times, and think it perfectly miraculous how it could have been.

WILLIAM BUCKLEY, 1852

WILLIAM BUCKLEY'S CLUB
George Serras, National Museum of Australia

SOURCES AND FURTHER READING: John Morgan, *The Life and Adventures of William Buckley*, Archibald MacDougall, Hobart, 1852, Reprint: Australian National University Press, Canberra, 1979.

Yoshinori Maeda
On loan from Yoshinori Maeda

Yoshinori Maeda
born 1932

YOSHINORI MAEDA ON BOARD A
PEARL LUGGER
On loan from Yoshinori Maeda

I was born on 1st May 1932 in Yutai, Ehime-Ken, Japan. My cousin, from the same town, Yutai, was presently working for a pearling company owned by Wally Scott in Broome. He had asked my brother Minoru Maeda to come and work for the same company, who had agreed to come to Broome. However, he had become engaged to marry and did not want to leave his fiancé. At the same time the company that I worked for in Osaka went into liquidation and I was unemployed. I agreed to take my brother's place in Australia. I arrived in Broome 22nd June 1955. For the first six months I was a trainee diver (called a 'try diver') then I was a diver for approximately 4–5 years. We went out to sea for 4–8 weeks at a time. The luggers had engines and three sails. Navigation was by compass only. We had no contact with shore people. Working/diving commenced just before sunrise and went till sunset, at least 12 hours a day Monday – Saturday. We never dived on Sundays. We stayed 45–50 minutes under water, on the deck for approximately 10 minutes whilst the lugger sailed back to the same area, and we dived again … There was great competition between boats to see who could collect the most shell. The divers were paid according to the amount of shell they collected … Shell was the lifeblood of the industry. Any natural pearls found were an additional bonus. It was estimated that one natural pearl was found for every 10,000 oysters.

I was diving at depths of over 20 fathoms. I had collected quite a lot of shell this day and so was working quite hard. I had tea and lay down, when I felt pain at about 7pm … I alerted the crew and they helped me into my diving gear and I went down to the original depth of about 23 fathoms. I had to stay at that depth for six hours. I tried coming up slowly, rising only about one foot, but the pain forced me down again. After around six hours, I was able to ascend to around 15 fathoms and stayed at that depth for about 24 hours. I was then able to slowly come up one fathom by one fathom until I was able to surface. I knew the time because the tenders gave a signal on the 'lifeline' rope at each hour. In all, I was under water for 36 hours. The lugger took me back to Broome … I stayed in Broome for a month, then went back to sea again.

I tried diving again. I was fine under 10 fathoms, but deeper than that, I felt sick again … The pain when you get the bends is very bad. I can't explain in words what it is like, but I had never before and never since had pain like that. I was diving at a depth of twelve fathoms and felt something pulling on my airpipe … I lost control of the air intake, the suit filled up with air and I turned upside down … The force was so great the thread on the screws holding the helmet shot off … I shot to the surface, but because of the weight of the shoes flipped over and went straight to the bottom again. The crew were pulling me up as fast as they could, but I had no breath left. The old divers used to tell us that if we were in danger of drowning, try to swallow water, it helps you last a bit longer. I had swallowed three times by the time the crew dragged me to the surface … when the crew started pulling in the air hose they found a huge mantaray was tangled in it. After diving I worked as an 'engineer' (looking after the engine) on the lugger. I married an Australian woman in 1969 and was naturalised in 1970. I now work for the Paspaley Pearling Company Pty Ltd doing maintenance on their buildings.

Yoshinori Maeda, 1999

DIVING HELMET, PASPALEY PEARLS
George Serras,
National Museum of Australia

SOURCES AND FURTHER READING: Yoshinori Maeda, written interview conducted by Kerrilyn Macpherson on behalf of the National Museum of Australia, 1999.

That's what we're like out here,
Beds of dried-up passions.

KENNETH SLESSOR, 1932

my jumper
    and her jumper
    are embracing
on the floor.

π.o. 2000

...obsession is a regionalism
of the mind.

Jay Davison 1972

Captivated by images, I was
drawn as a child to historic
portraits of children, and
developed a passion for
exploring the innocence of
the past. I discovered my
deepest passion in the love
I have for my daughter.

CARMEL BIRD, 2000

So I, who bless
Your hot and passionate ways,
Still need the starry loves
Of virgin days.

LESBIA HARFORD, 1917

My lust's not filthy. It's natural.
Makes me feel good. Like the
rain ... and the rivers runnin'
when everything's dead and
dry, up here.

KATHARINE SUSANNAH PRICHARD, 1927

'Tis strange how often the
men out back will take to
some curious craft,
Some ruling passion to
keep their thoughts away
from the overdraft;

AB PATERSON, 1902

No grand enterprise is ever achieved
without passion. Passion breathes life
into it, passion protects it and passion
sustains it. And even when it's
finished, passion hangs around,
unwilling to leave, eyes wide saying
'Wow!' over and over again.

Drew Tod 2000

passi

passion

Passion, like love, attracts and is attractive.
Full of longing and desire, a passion for someone or
something — intense love or an outburst of anger —
can become so strong it's *barely* controllable.
If you feed this raw appetite, passion can tip into
obsession. Once aroused, in all its fervent keenness,
passion can be something to relish.

FRANCESCA RENDLE-SHORT, 2000

The emotion of affection is
not less genuine than love.

PATRICK WHITE, 1970

Gardens should be portioned off for all
lovers in the spring and early summer
where they should be allowed to give
themselves up, in a religious spirit, to
the consummation of their love.

WJ CHIDLEY, 1915

But 210 years is not short.
Not if we think of it in terms
of lives lived and of all the
events and activities and
passionate involvements
that went into those lives.

DAVID MALOUF, 1998

It's the world's only defence,
that we hurt out of love,
not out of hate.

RANDOLPH STOW, 1958

There is no passion like the first!

HENRY THOMAS KENDALL, 1869

Alan Puckett
Gregory McBean

Trained in fine arts at Yale University, Alan Puckett came to Australia from North Carolina in 1956 looking for a way to escape the straightjacket of American business culture.

ALAN PUCKETT'S ART WORK FROM THE 1970s
Warren Penny

The early years here were good working years. The printing techniques of both magazines and newspapers were very poor, and photographs reproduced badly, so everything was drawn in ads. I was pretty hot drawing hard objects, cars, refrigerators, etc, and so cracked the market. Early sixties I got into photo-retouching.

Around this time, late sixties, I'd got into doing illustrations, mainly airbrush. The ad agencies went all retro fifties and the airbrush was king.

The seventies were spent living, breathing, racing motorcycles.

The seventies were what I'd call my hippie years. I teamed up with an extremely talented photographer and graphic designer and we started working on a book about classic motorbikes. We were sick of being slaves to the ad business so we dropped out and started custom painting Harleys and surfie Vans. Wonderful! We could paint whatever wild stuff we felt like, nude chicks being molested by monsters, the perfect wave with board rider locked in the tube. A lot of it was seventies cliché but I had a freedom I'd never had before (or since).

I think the first effort I did was on a chap's Harley Davidson with a side car and we were using acrylic lacquer which was a common automotive paint system back in that time, and that was ideal for this kind of work because it is very fast drying and it goes through an air brush very well.

You'd be doing something for some tattooed gentleman on his Harley, you see, always big guys on Harleys, always large, and while the work was going on they would rumble up the lane here. Thirty guys on Harleys to see the progress of the work. It was absolutely wonderful. I wonder what the neighbours thought.

The eighties? Gave up smoking dope, got a haircut, put on a suit and started back in advert illustrations, did some good stuff too. The good jobs, from my point of view artistically, have dried up from the mid nineties. Trouble of being a realist artist is the computer can do it better.

ALAN PUCKETT, 1998

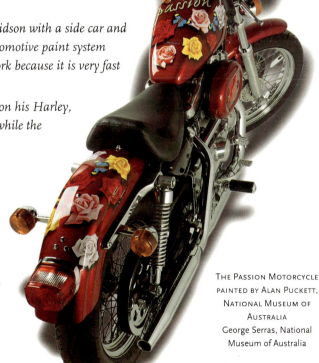

THE PASSION MOTORCYCLE PAINTED BY ALAN PUCKETT, NATIONAL MUSEUM OF AUSTRALIA
George Serras, National Museum of Australia

SOURCES AND FURTHER READING: Alan Puckett, letter to Constance and Jack, 1998, Alan Puckett Collection, National Museum of Australia.

GEOFF KING
Mark Thomson

112

Geoff King's shed is in suburban Adelaide.

*I think that's one of the things about Australia. A 'man and his
shed' is part of our lifestyle and I think any man that hasn't got a
shed is missing out greatly.*

*I think it is important to have a shed because from that little square
tin shed you can build something.*

*The shed is part of the family — it's part of my life — it's an
institution of its own.*

*The things that you put aside, you hang them up in the shed
because somewhere down the track you may want to use it and sure
enough the old things that you were going to throw away years ago
become so important today.*

THE INTERIOR OF GEOFF KING'S SHED
Mark Thomson

*Sheds in Australia are part of the Australian icon. It's a quiet little
area of your own, no-one interrupts you. No-one comes down and starts to tell you what to do. You can shut your door
and your shed becomes your own little domain, like a little secret place in a way.*

*The jobs that I do in the shed basically are ones that you can make something, repair it, pull it to pieces again, modify
it, try it again, and that's what makes it worthwhile. You can leave it, come back to it, because no-one is going to go
into your shed, it's your little private property. No-one goes in and moves it because you can leave it there for a week, for
a month, but when you go back it's still sitting on that bench where you left it in your shed — which you couldn't do in
the house.*

My shed is really my domain, mine and my dogs.

*The shed is part of my life now I've retired. It's because I can walk out there
and spend an hour in the shed and just lull away the time and do little
things at my pace, at my leisure. I have mates drop in. It's like a little
meeting place, really, the old shed. We've got a couple of old chairs and
stools in there. My old mates come in and we sit down and have a bit of a
natter and talk about what he was doing in his shed or what I've been
doing and that way it's really part of a conversation — it's part of your
lifestyle today.*

*From the time I was a young lad I've always loved telephones. I don't
know why. I think it's just that you get a fascination for something when
you start to collect it. For the last 40 years I've done nothing but collect
phones and put them together and find the broken pieces and repair them.*

*I've always had a love for the Australian phone. Our own engineers in
the department here, PMG days, designed this little phone called the
Australian 237. It's a beautiful little telephone, little wooden one. It's
always had a bit of a soft spot in my heart because it's typically Australian.
Something we made during our darkest hours.*

GEOFF KING, 1999

TELEPHONE RESTORED BY GEOFF KING, GEOFF KING
George Serras, National Museum of Australia

SOURCES AND FURTHER READING: Geoff King, oral history interview with Sophie Jensen, 17 November 1999, National Museum of Australia;
Mark Thomson, *The Mini Book of Blokes and Sheds*, Angus and Robertson, Sydney, 1998.

IRENE CHATFIELD
On loan from Irene Chatfield

Passion Irene Chatfield
born 1949

In 1989 the Victorian Football League (VFL) announced that two football clubs, the Footscray Bulldogs and the Fitzroy Lions, were to merge in a 'secret deal'. Irene took the VFL to court. Today, however, they are the Western Bulldogs.

IRENE CHATFIELD AT THE FOOTBALL
Peta Clancy

When I was born Mum said the girls can barrack for Footscray and the boys can barrack for Carlton for Dad, but Dad was unlucky, my brothers are Richmond and North Melbourne. My sister is also a Mighty Bulldogs supporter. Since I was around 5 years old I have liked Footscray. When I was 11 years old I started going to football regularly. I couldn't wait for Saturdays to come. It was enjoyment to go some way to see my team play. By the time I was 17 or 18 I loved them, I wanted to be part of the club. I used to sit in the outer and say to my family and friends, one day I'll be a part of this club, and they'd say, sure Irene.

As a fan of my mighty club, I collect badges, I love to show our players off on my scarf, and they look for their badge on my scarf. I have had players say to me, I have made the scarf, that's good, and the players say to each other while I'm there about some of them when they first started, how they looked then with their long hair and they have a laugh.

I don't think I'm any different from any other fan, we all love our football and our clubs. I guess I was just lucky to become a big part of my club, I was in the right spot at the right time, I was a member of my club the Bulldogs and we were going under, I wanted to be there to help in some way, I wanted to help my players and I was lucky. I was there when they needed me. They, the players, have given me so much over the years, they have given me something in life to look forward to, somewhere to go and enjoy myself, have fun and laugh. It was great to give them something — their club.

I went to court because they had not consulted the members about the merger. When it was announced I got on radio the very next morning pleading with all Bulldog supporters to get down to our club and protest, show our strength. That they can't do this to our club, and within the hour there were hundreds of supporters at our mighty club to save them and save them we did.

I was presented with that guernsey by the trainers and the mighty support staff. I keep it as my special souvenir because it means so much to me. For them to care about giving me something.

IRENE CHATFIELD, 1999

IRENE CHATFIELD'S WESTERN BULLDOG'S SCARF, IRENE CHATFIELD
George Serras, National Museum of Australia

SOURCES AND FURTHER READING: Irene Chatfield, written interview with Johanna Parker, 1999, National Museum of Australia; Kevin Sheedy and Carolyn Brown, *Football's Women: The Forgotten Heroes*, Penguin Books, Ringwood, Vic, 1998.

MARGARET GROSVENOR
National Museum of Australia

Sixteen-year-old Margaret Grosvenor made her debut at the annual Masonic Debutante Ball held in Broken Hill, NSW, in 1959.

On the night there was a great sense of excitement mixed with terror — that we'd stumble in the curtsy or over our partner's feet or get our feet tangled in the delicate fabric of unaccustomed long dresses. But overwhelmingly there was a sense of feeling special, beautiful, lifted beyond our everyday lives. That it might have been a little bizarre following a ritual from the London season in outback Australia certainly never crossed our minds.

It was a magical night. I guess my own special memory is of the romance — being taken home for the first time by my boyfriend (who had also got a dinner suit for the occasion) rather than by my partner who was a good friend. My parents were not impressed.

As for life around this time, we were all supposed to be studying for the Leaving Certificate before leaving the Hill definitively — for Teachers' College or University. But the routine at school was broken by the odd Deb Ball or 21st given by the outbackers, and by plans for the School Ball and Farewell to Fifth Year. Friday nights were important. We all went to the Y — YWCA for girls, YMCA for boys — and met up afterwards at the milk bar. Saturdays were for football and Sundays for Church and Sunday School — and who's to say you couldn't have a little flirtation there.

The dress was a froth of tulle with a ruched fitted top and a mass of petticoats — seven, I think. The accessories were almost as important: the long Merry Widow bra with suspenders and 15 denier stockings, the delicate lace-trimmed nylon pants, the long white gloves, the little beaded bag, the white furry cape, even special bath salts. It took months acquiring it all. And on the night the little silver and pearl necklace from my parents, and bracelet from my partner. I felt like a princess — transformed from the schoolgirl in the heavy serge uniform.

MARGARET GROSVENOR (POCOCK), 1999

MARGARET GROSVENOR IN HER DEBUTANTE DRESS
National Museum of Australia

MARGARET GROSVENOR AT HER DEBUT
National Museum of Australia

SOURCES AND FURTHER READING: Margaret Grosvenor (Pocock), written interview with Johanna Parker, 4 July 1999, National Museum of Australia.

MONTE PUNSHON
Kobe Japan–Australia Society

Monte Punshon
1882–1989

Monte Punshon came out publicly as a lesbian at the age of 104. Her life spanned many changes for women. Monte held a lifelong passion for Asian cultures. She learnt Mandarin and Japanese in the 1930s. During the Second World War she worked as a warden at the Tatura Internment Camp near Shepparton in north-east Victoria looking after the non-English-speaking Japanese prisoners. Many years later she was invited to Japan and publicly thanked for her friendship and kindness to the internees. She was an unconventional woman in many ways.

Japanese internees at Tatura, Victoria, celebrate a wedding
Kobe Japan–Australia Society

What's wrong with being in love? Love attracts me, and love is attractive ... And you've got to be in love. In love with life, or in love with something or someone, but you've got to be in love!

MONTE PUNSHON, 1987

When I was younger I felt a great attraction to women always, much more so than men, women meant quite a lot to me and men were just men and that was all. Well Debbie was a wonderful friend of mine and she also was very go ahead and independent in nature. She was so kind and so loving towards all women particularly, yes it was a wonderful friendship.

I enjoy every minute of the period in which I can hear of women being caught up in politics, in affairs of the nation, in happenings of the world and adventures, women going round the world solo and following their own desires and wishes. I think women have become very much more powerful and worthwhile in the last 10 years.

Once when women were not married they were looked upon as being on the shelf and somewhat inferior and people were sorry for them, but gradually and now particularly they are positively glad, some of them, that they are not pressured into being married. They prefer to be single on their own, people not just appendages, and having the vote is something quite wonderful. They have a say in political matters and in their own lives and altogether they are an entirely different creation.

MONTE PUNSHON, 1988

Japanese kimono presented to Monte Punshon, Margaret Taylor
George Serras, National Museum of Australia

SOURCES AND FURTHER READING: Monte Punshon, 'In love with a memory', in Margaret Bradstock and Louise Wakeling (eds), *Words from the Same Heart*, Hale and Iremonger, Sydney, 1987; Monte Punshon, interview, 1988, *A Single Life: Ethel May 'Monte' Punshon, 1882–1989, Australian Women's Archival Project*, 1991, APECK Productions, directed by Nancy Peck, produced by Sue Maslin; Ethel May (Monte) Punshon, *Monte-San: The Times Between, Life Lies Hidden*, Kobe Japan–Australia Society, Kobe, Japan, 1987.

Acknowledgments and sources

The *Eternity* exhibition was developed by the following team at the National Museum of Australia: Dr Marion Stell, Sophie Jensen, Johanna Parker, Allison Cadzow and Zoe Greenwood. Many other staff contributed to the exhibition in different ways.

The exhibition writer was Francesca Rendle-Short.

I wish to thank both Greg Andrews and Dr Stephen Foster at the National Museum of Australia for their encouragement of this publication.

Where necessary, some quotations within stories have been edited for the purposes of continuity.

The following people generously assisted with the stories in *Eternity*.

Cliff Butcher, Gabriel Gallery, Gundagai; Caleb Williams, Justice and Police Museum, Sydney; Dr Michelle Potter; Barbara Cuckson; Robert Vasey, Canberra; Associate Professor Joy Damousi, Melbourne; Donna Ives, Vasey Housing, Sydney; Pearl Hamaguchi, Broome; Grant Sellwood; Mark Bin Bakar, Broome; Sister Leone Collins, Broome; Julie Martin, JS Battye Library of West Australian History; Lindy Chamberlain-Creighton; Rick Creighton; Jean Locke, Boulia; Chris Blanch, Boulia Shire Council; Jason Webb, Promotion Pictures, Queensland; Tim the Yowie Man; Nicholas Holt; Jean Clough, Nepean Historical Society Inc, Victoria; Elizabeth Bernard, Carolyn Laffan, Performing Arts Museum, Victorian Arts Centre; Kent Blackmore, Sydney; Madeleine Scully, Museum of the Riverina, Wagga Wagga; Claire Campbell, Wagga Wagga Regional Library; Alan Ventress, Chris Pryke, State Library of New South Wales; Margot Riley, State Library of New South Wales; Patricia Worthington, NSW; Betty Cuthbert, Western Australia; Nita Lawes-Gilvear, Youngtown; Anne Killalea, Mount Nelson; Peter Wood and the Wood family; Gavin Souter; Philippa Quinn, Australian Broadcasting Corporation; Rosie Cross; Técha Noble; Rob Joyner jr; Imogen Ashlee; Pedro Altuna; Lisa Pears; Monika Jansch; Gwen Meredith, Bowral; Geoff Harris, ABC Document Archives; Heather Rose, Adelaide; Christopher Corin, South Australia Film Corporation; Rolf de Heer, Adelaide; Elizabeth Bernard, Carolyn Laffan, Performing Arts Museum, Victorian Arts Centre; Samuel Harry Van Der Sluice; Paul Field; Paula Dunn; Therese Skinner; Greg Page; Anthony Field; Murray Cook; Jeff Fatt; Peter Castrission, Pat Jeffress and the Castrission family; Nick Loukissas, Niagara Café; Professor Bob Gollan, Canberra; Envoy (Dr) George Hazell and Robyn Edge, The Salvation Army Heritage Centre, Sydney; Elaine Spence; Mick Strawbridge, Bridgewater, SA; Noelle Sandwith, Brighton, UK; Normie Rowe, Chris Cunningham, John Wilkie, Lou Butcher and Mick van Poeteren, Vietnam Veterans Motorcycle Club; David Vretchkoff, Sydney; Harrow Surfboards, Sydney; Joan Russell, Adelaide; Jill Cassidy, Queen Victoria Museum and Art Gallery; Beverly Robinson, Melbourne; Lyle Tuttle, San Francisco Tattoo Museum; Reg Mombassa, Sydney; Martina O'Doherty, Sydney; Mambo Graphics, Sydney; Ron Muncaster, Sydney; Jane Becker, Workshop Production Manager, Sydney Gay and Lesbian Mardi Gras; Benny Zable; Faith Bandler, Sydney; Sister M Benedetta and the Sisters of St Joseph of the Sacred Heart, North Sydney; Sister Claire Ahern; Carol Hetherington, University of Queensland; Audrey Johnson; Robyn Archer; Rachel Skinner, Rick Raftos Management, Sydney; Vasiliki Nihas; Dr Geza Varasdi and the Varasdi family; Maria Tence, Immigration Museum, Melbourne; Kim Eastman; Susie Aulich; Kate Cliff; Gaynor Peaty; Denise Pilkington; Mary Lee and the Lee family, Darwin; Bill Brassell, Australian War Memorial; Toni Roberston, Sydney; Virginia Coventry, Sydney; Dr Ann Genovese, Justice Research Centre, Sydney; Robert Lawry, NSW Parliamentary Archives; Dr Christine Allison, Saffron Walden Museum, UK; John Ross; Michael McCarthy, Western Australian Maritime Museum; Yoshinori Maeda, Broome; Nicholas Paspaley, Paspaley Pearls; Kerrilyn Macpherson, Paspaley Pearls, Broome; Kali Wilde, Sydney; Fiona Coote, Sydney; Alan Puckett, Sydney; Geoff King; Dulcie King; Mark Thomson, Adelaide; Irene Chatfield; Western Bulldogs Football Club; Australian Football League; Meg Pocock, Sydney; Margaret Taylor; Ruth Ford; Sue Maslin.

Extracts from the following texts have been quoted in the exhibition theme introductions:

SEPARATION

David Malouf, *A Spirit of Play: The Making of Australian Consciousness*, ABC Books, Sydney, 1998; Elizabeth Macarthur, quoted in R Therry, *Reminiscences of Thirty Years' Residence in New South Wales and Victoria*, London, 1863; Rosemary Dobson, from the poem 'The Gods', *Collected Poems*, Angus and Robertson, Sydney, 1991; Watkin Tench, *Settlement at Port Jackson*, 1793; Oodgeroo Noonuccal, from the poem 'Last of His Tribe', *My People: A Kath Walker Collection*, Jacaranda Press, Milton, Qld, 1970; Henry Handel Richardson, *The Way Home*, Heinemann, London, 1925; Robert Dessaix, commissioned quote, 2000; Tom Flood, commissioned quote, 2000; Boori Pryor and Meme McDonald, commissioned quote, 1999; George Johnston, *Clean Straw for Nothing*, Collins, London, 1964.

MYSTERY

Patrick White, *The Tree of Man*, Eyre and Spottiswoode, London, 1955; EB Mackennal, *Art in Australia*, June 1927; Mary E Fullerton, *Australia and Other Essays*, 1928; Eleanor Dark, *The Timeless Land*, Macmillan, New York, 1941; Fergus Hume, *Mystery of a Hansom Cab*, 1886; Beth Yahp, commissioned quote, 2000; Robert Adamson, commissioned quote, 2000; Patrick White, *The Tree of Man*, Eyre and Spottiswoode, London, 1955.

HOPE

Colin Johnson/Mudrooroo Narogin, *Wild Cat Falling*, Angus and Robertson, Sydney, 1965; Henry Lawson, *Verses Popular and Humorous*, 1900; Dr Ruby Langford Ginibi, commissioned quote, 2000; Christos Tsiolkas, commissioned quote, 2000; Anonymous, *Old Bush Songs*, 1905; Adam Lindsay Gordon, *Miscellaneous Poems*, 1893; King O'Malley, *Commonwealth Parliamentary Debates*, 8 October 1903; Frederic Manning, *Her Privates We*, Davies, London, 1929.

JOY

Henry Parkes, *The Beautiful Terrorist and Other Poems*, 1885; Sir Joseph Banks, *Endeavour Journal*, 1770; Caroline Leakey (Oline Keese), *Broad Arrow*, 1900; Chris Wallace-Crabbe, from the poem 'A Wintry Manifesto', 1963; Roy Wright, *Age*, 26 January 1983; Guy Eden from the poem 'Victor Trumper', c.1900; Ethel C Pedley, *Dot and the Kangaroo*, 1906; James McAuley, from the poem 'To Any Poet', *Australian Poets*, Angus and Robertson, Sydney, 1963; Judith Wright, from the poem 'The Surfer', *Five Senses*, Angus and Robertson, Sydney, 1963; Suneeta Peres da Costa, commissioned quote, 2000; Tim Winton, *Cloudstreet*, McPhee Gribble, Ringwood, Vic, 1991; Susan Hampton, commissioned quote, 1998.

LONELINESS

Marcus Clarke, *Australian Tales*, 1896; Kylie Tennant, *Ride on Stranger*, Angus and Robertson, Sydney, 1943; M Barnard Eldershaw, *My Australia*, Jarolds, London, 1939; Barrett Reid, from the poem 'Nothing', *Making Country*, Angus and Robertson, Sydney, 1995; Judith Wright, from the poem 'The Company of Lovers', *The Moving Image*, Meanjin Press, Melbourne, 1946; Jackie Huggins, commissioned quote, 2000; Gillian Mears, commissioned quote, 1997; Rodney Hall, commissioned quote, 2000.

THRILL

T McCombie, *Adventure of a Colonist*, 1845; WH Christie, *Love Story by a Bushman*, 1841; Dorothy Hewett, from the poem 'Living Dangerously', *Collected Poems 1940–1995*, Fremantle Arts Centre Press, South Fremantle, 1995; Caroline Leakey (Oline Keese), *Broad Arrow*, 1900; Lennie Lower, *Here's Another*, Frank C Johnson and Co, Sydney, 1932; Ada Cambridge, *The Hand in the Dark*, 1913; Annamarie Jagose, commissioned quote, 2000; Dorothy Porter, from the poem 'Music', *Crete*, Hyland House, South Melbourne, 1996; William Morris Hughes, 1940s, quoted in John Thompson, *On the Lips of Living Men*, Lansdowne Press, Melbourne, 1962; Ada Cambridge, *Unspoken Thoughts*, 1887; Linda Jaivin, *Eat me*, Text Publishing, Melbourne, 1995; Harry Hooton, from the poem 'A Sweet Disorder in the Dress', *Collected Poems*, Angus and Robertson, Sydney, 1990.

DEVOTION

Harold Begbie, from the poem 'Britons Beyond the Seas', c.1900; Dorothy Hewett, *Wild Card*, McPhee Gribble, Ringwood, Vic, 1990; Ada Cambridge, *The Hand in the Dark*, 1913; Sue Woolfe, commissioned quote, 1996; Chris Wallace-Crabbe, commissioned quote, 2000; Lloyd Ross, from the article 'The politics of the Depression', in *Economic Record*, vol 8, December 1932; Mary Gilmore, from the poem 'The Woman', *Selected Verse*, Angus and Robertson, Sydney, 1948; Mary Hannay Foott, *Where the Pelican Builds*, 1885.

FEAR

Marcus Clarke, *Australian Tales*, 1896; Phillip Law, from the *Medical Journal of Australia*, 20 February 1960; Frank Kellaway, from the poem 'Dead Cow', c.1970; Patrick White, *Voss*, Viking, New York, 1957; Henry Lawson, *In the Days When the World Was Wide*, 1912; Carol Novack, from the poem 'You Try To Get Out of the Fear', *Living Alone without a Dictionary*, Makar Press, St Lucia, Qld, 1974; Patricia Sykes, commissioned quote, 2000; Melissa Lucashenko, Murri woman from Brisbane, commissioned quote, 2000.

CHANCE

Donald Horne, *The Lucky Country*, Harmondsworth, Penguin, 1964; AB Paterson, *The Man from Snowy River and Other Verses*, 1891; Ian Bevan, *The Sunburnt Country*, Collins, London, 1954; CJ Dennis, from the poem 'Mar', *The Songs of the Sentimental Bloke*, 1915; Roy Rene, *Mo's Memoirs*, Reed and Harris, Melbourne, 1945; Dorothy Hewett, from the poem 'Alice in Wormland', 1987; Kate Grenville, commissioned quote, 2000; Kylie Tennant, *Ride on Stranger*, Angus and Robertson, Sydney, 1943; CJ Dennis, from the poem 'A Spring Song', *The Songs of a Sentimental Bloke*, 1915; Frank Hardy, *The Yarns of Billy Borker*, AH and AW Reed, Sydney, 1965.

PASSION

Jim Davidson, *Westerly*, no 4, 1978; Lesbia Harford, 1917, from the poem 'You May Have Other Loves', 6.9.17; Patrick White, *The Vivisector*, Cape, London, 1970; Katharine Susannah Prichard, *Brumby Innes*, Paterson's Press, Perth, 1927; WJ Chidley, *The Answer*, D Smith, Sydney, 1915; Randolph Stow, *To the Islands*, Macdonald, London, 1958; AB Paterson, *Rio Grande's Last Race and Other Verses*, 1902; David Malouf, *A Spirit of Play: The Making of Australian Consciousness*, ABC Books, Sydney, 1998; Carmel Bird, commissioned quote, 2000; Mem Fox, commissioned quote, 2000; π.O., commissioned quote, 2000; Kenneth Slessor, from the poem 'Talbingo', *Collected Poems*, Angus and Robertson, Sydney, 1994; Henry Thomas Kendall, *Leaves from Australian Forests*, 1869.

The following general sources are also acknowledged: Stephen Murray-Smith, *The Dictionary of Australian Quotations*, Heinemann, Richmond, Vic, 1984; The University of Sydney Library, Scholarly Electronic Text and Image Service, http://setis.library.usyd.edu.au.

Commissioned quotes were selected by Francesca Rendle-Short.